Poetry Explorers

Yorkshire

Edited by Claire Tupholme

First published in Great Britain in 2009 by

Young Writers

Remus House
Coltsfoot Drive
Peterborough
PE2 9JX
Telephone: 01733 890066
Website: www.youngwriters.co.uk

All Rights Reserved
Book Design by Spencer Hart
Illustrations by Ali Smith
© Copyright Contributors 2009
SB ISBN 978-1-84924-259-2

Foreword

At Young Writers our defining aim is to promote an enjoyment of reading and writing amongst children and young adults. By giving aspiring poets the opportunity to see their work in print, their love of the written word as well as confidence in their own abilities has the chance to blossom.

Our latest competition Poetry Explorers was designed to introduce primary school children to the wonders of creative expression. They were given free reign to write on any theme and in any style, thus encouraging them to use and explore a variety of different poetic forms.

We are proud to present the resulting collection of regional anthologies which are an excellent showcase of young writing talent. With such a diverse range of entries received, the selection process was difficult yet very rewarding. From comical rhymes to poignant verses, there is plenty to entertain and inspire within these pages. We hope you agree that this collection bursting with imagination is one to treasure.

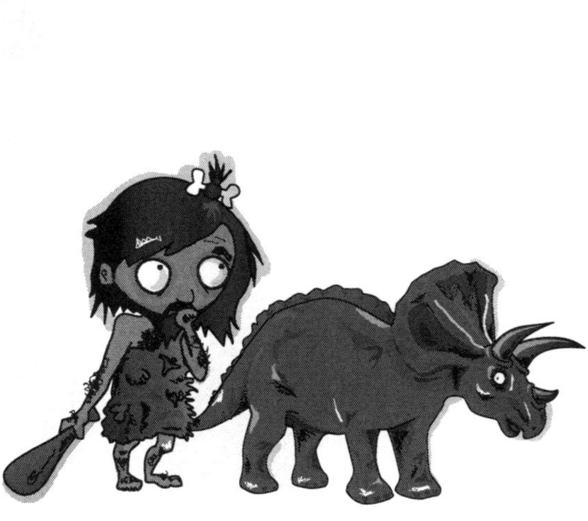

Contents

Beeford CE (VC) Primary School, Beeford
Oliver Morley 1
Charlotte Alderson (11) 2
Liam Kelly (11) 3
Thomas Gordge 4
Zak Mayo 5
Javi Rochelle (10) 6

Bilton Grange CP School, Harrogate
Gareth Harris (9) 6
Chloe Marshall (10) 7
Nicola Williams (10) 7
Matthew Craig-Ramsden (9) 8
Chavy Mtawali (10) 8
Roisin Swainston-Rainford (10) 9
Joseph Atkinson (9) 9
Ki-Ten Pat Lorridana-Atkinson (10) 10
Reece Campbell (9) 10
Phoebe Hanslow (10) 11
Lottie Willmore (9) 11
Kyle Wallace (10) 12
Amy Noble (10) 12
Katalin Holstead (10) 13
Cameron Phillips (9) 13
Lewis Parker (10) 14
Catherine Greenham (9) 14

Cawood CE (VA) Primary School, Selby
Ellie Croft (11) 15
Ellen Dethridge (10) 16
Jacob Linley (11) 17
Luke Royle (10) 18
Harriet McCowliff (11) 18
Rosie Hutton (11) 19
Sam Cheetham (10) 19
Lizzie Langdale (10) 20

William Dennis (11) 20
Eve Bray (10) 21
Ellie Edwards (11) 21
Emma Howie (10) 22

High Bentham CP School, High Bentham
Nathan Jeffs (9) 22
Rosie Fletcher (10) 23
Charlotte Green (10) 24
Amy Lawson (9) 25
William Jackson (10) 25
Aimee Read (10) 26
Calum Cochrane (9) 26
Lauren Atkinson (10) 27
Bethany Jenkins (9) 27
Elliott Andrews (10) 27

Menston Primary School, Menston
Ella Mortimer (11) 28
Sophie Robinson (9) 29
Martha Whitaker (9) 30
Lucy Turner (10) 30
Bradley Brown (10) 31
Stacy Ramsey (10) 32
Tom Luxton (10) 33
Millie Baxter (9) 34
Gemma Wright (9) 35
Robbie Hirst (9) 36
Kezia Finch (9) 37
Sam Simons (10) 38
Robbie Sandground (9) 39
Tom Palmer (10) 40
Katie-Rose Mortimer (9) 41
Jamie Jerome (9) 41
Anna Middleton (9) 42
Ellie Benn (10) 42
Abigail Spencer (9) 43

Maria Sage (7) 43	James Myers (9) 65
Phoebe Walker (8) 44	Miles Charlesworth (9) 65
Jack Hargreaves (10) 44	Stanley Fleming (9) 66
Alice Jackson (8) 45	Max McNeil (9) 66
Jonathan Britton (10) 45	Harriet Jackson (10) 67
Aimee Palmer (10) 46	Oliver Gibbs (10) 67
James Hill (8) 46	Oliver Mordey (9) 68
Grace Malir (10) 47	Phoebe Connor (10) 68
Joe Westwood (9) 47	Georgia Forder (9) 69
Rory Haggart (11) 48	Emily Lloyd (9) 69
Mary Slack (10) 48	Thomas Jackson (10) 70
Benjamin Lulham-Robinson (10) 49	Joseph Tindall (11) 70
Sophie Benn (8) 49	Callum Clarke (8) 71
Jacob Knowland (10) 50	Charlie Kinsman (8) 71
David Bulcock (9) 50	Hugh Berry (9) 72
Milly Brown (10) 51	Josh Hargreaves (10) 72
Joe Woollin (8) 51	Oliver Haggart (9) 73
Alessandra Ricci (8) 52	Ruby Richmond (9) 73
Harry Watson (7) 52	Alfie Tennant (9) 74
Lucy Campbell (9) 53	Jack Smith (11) 74
Toby Berry (10) 53	Mark Wharrier (10) 75
Nathan Twigg (9) 54	Harry Myers (10) 75
Holly Margerrison (11) 54	Harry Cooper (10) 76
Benedict Lane (10) 55	Adam France (9) 76
Francis Westhead (8) 55	Riyah Chhokar & Ella Sanderson (9) ... 77
Jonathan Lupton (10) 56	Michaela Devlin (7) 77
Ashley Gomersall (10) 56	Léona McLoughlin (9) 78
Charlotte Borwell (11) 57	Dhugal Sandground (7) 78
Holly Ramsey (9) 57	Charley Smith (9) 79
Bradley Burrows (9) 58	Melissa Redmond (9) 79
Robert Westwood (10) 58	Grace Slack (9) 80
Isabelle Hill (11) 59	Ellie Wilson (11) 80
Tom Kirkham (8) 59	George Cooper (8) 81
Eleanor Freeman (10) 60	Tarragon Huddleston (11) 81
Tommy Hinchliff (10) 60	William Hargreaves (8) 82
Elizabeth Westhead (10) 61	Ben Kirkham (8) 82
Erin Shaw (7) 61	Emily Robson (9) 83
Seb Lane (8) 62	Kate Hargreaves (8) 83
Hazel Bate (11) 62	Gabriel O'Hooley (11) 84
Rebecca Clarke (8) 63	Josephine Gibbs (8) 84
Ellie Myers (10) 63	Daniel Aitken (7) 85
James Turland (10) 64	Rosie Brown (8) 85
Olivia Deacon (8) 64	Sam Gulley (9) 85

Jake Holberry (9) 86
Rufus O'Hooley (8) 86
Daniel Ryan (10) 86
Molly Settle (8) 87
Fiona Moore (7) 87
Olivia Thomas (9) 87

Norton Community Primary School, Norton

Amber Barratt (11) 88
Anna Hubery (11) 89
Nathan Welham (10) 90
Harry Edwards (10) 90
Adam Peel (10) 91
Marcus Brigham (11) 91
Daniel Cockerill (11) 92
Grace Milner (10) 92
Kieran Cook (10) 93
Emma Piercy (10) 93
Christopher Bean (10) 94
Jodie Hawes (11) 94
Sophie Mort (10) 95
Charlotte Johnson (11) 95
Lianna Hart (10) 96
Lauren Clifford (10) 96
Rebekah Bell (11) 97
Imogen Barnes (10) 97
Caleb Barratt (11) 98
Oscar Johnston (10) 98
Kiera Colgan (11) 98
Nikita Daffern (11) 99
Cameron Coulthard (10) 99
Stevie Hamilton (11) 99
Heather Robinson (10) 100
Rhys Douthwaite (11) 100
Joshua Downing (10) 100

St Mary's RC Primary School, Malton

Joseph Wing (11) 101
Ellen Longworth (10) 102
Mary Rice (10) 102
Thomas Wing (11) 103

Callum Young (11) 103
Daniela Horne (11) 104

St Peter's RC Primary School, Scarborough

Joe Harrison (10) 104
Georgia Ward (9) 105
Alex Duncan (10) 106
Abigail Kimmitt (9) 107
James Brown (10) 108
James Pilmer (10) 109
Matthew Cottle (10) 110
Ella Gridley (10) 111
Jacob Ratcliffe (9) 112
Jenny Scott (9) 113
Rebecca Guy (10) 114
Scott Brierley (10) 115
Tiffany Harrison (10) 115
Chloé Moran (10) 116
Michelle Sunico (10) 116
Angus Polkey (10) 117
Eleanor Regan (10) 117

Southcoates Primary School, Hull

Sophie Walker (9) 118
Hannah Townend (7) 118
Amy Watkin (9) 119
Shanice Bell (8) 119
Connor Thompson (8) 120
Ellie Danville (8) 120
Jessica Wilkinson (9) 120

Stakesby Primary School, Whitby

Megan Idle 121
Alfie Swales 121
Yasmin Dimbleby (8) 122
Tilly Swales (9) 122
Charlotte Wharrick (9) 123
Helena Graham (9) 123
Henry Atkinson (9) 124
Amy Porteus (9) 124

Joe Beeforth (9) 125
Fleur Waring (8) 125
Kaitlin Swales 125

Swainby & Potto CE Primary School, Swainby

Jake Brown (8) 126
Bethany Morgan (11) 127
Ryan Beadle (10) 127
Jona Turner (9) & William Howes (11) 128
Thomas Stevens (9) 129
Joe McKenna (7) 130
Kate Stevens (11) 131
Elle Harrison (8) 132
Jade Keetley (8) 132
Zoe Ralston (10) 133

Thorpepark Primary School, Hull

Kyra Pymer (10) 133
Danielle Johnson (10) 134
Luke Hall (10) 134
Dana Lowther (10) 135
Scott Morfitt (10) 135
Shannon Heath (10) 136
Macauley Watts (9) 136
Cameron Waters (10) 137
Adam Rumkee (11) 137
Nathan Lawler (10) 138
Jade Jackson (11) 138
Matthew Richards (10) 139
Ellie Humphrey (10) 139
Joanne Charlton (11) 140
Jordan Hall (10) 140

Tilbury Primary School, Hull

Georgie Taylor & Kara Calvert (10) 141
Bethany Harper & Hollie Toft (10) 142
Oliver Bradley (9), Owen Fullard &
Matthew Burgess (10) 142
Elisha-Mae Jones (9) 143

The Poems

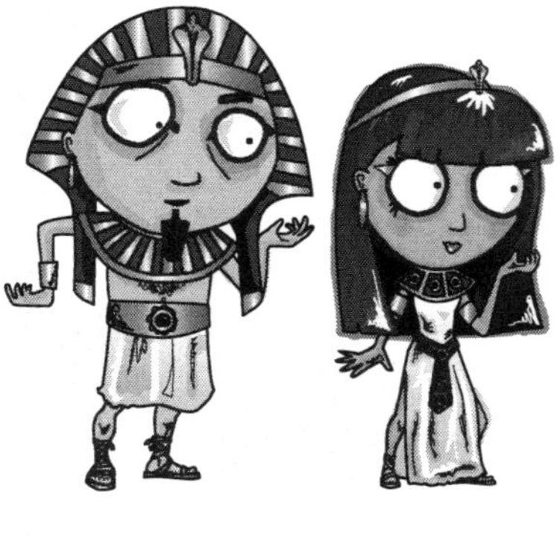

Untitled

(Inspired by 'A Poem to be Spoken Silently' by Pie Corbett)

It was so quiet that I heard,
my sister's Barbie doll tantruming -
she didn't have the right shoes …

It was so still I heard
the cups gossiping and whispering
about the events of the day …

It was so calm I heard
the moon chatting
to distant stars …

It was so silent I heard
my pillow moaning
'Get off me …'

It was so peaceful I heard
the flowers nudge
and tell each other to wake up …

It was so quiet I heard
Jack Frost lie down
with his ice-cold blanket …

It was so calm I heard
the chimney cough as smoke billowed out …

It was so calm I could hear
pollution murdering the world
step by step …

Oliver Morley
Beeford CE (VC) Primary School, Beeford

A Poem To Be Spoken Silently

(Inspired by 'A Poem to be Spoken Silently' by Pie Corbett)

It was so silent that I heard,
the snow punching its way,
for the best patch of grass …

It was so quiet that I could hear,
the dolls arguing over
the best frill dress
to wear the next day …

It was so peaceful I could hear,
the green, fat caterpillar chomping,
the green fat cabbage leaves in the vegetable patch …

It was so calm I heard
my shelf moaning about my books, 'Shuffle over a bit …'
It was so still I heard
the carpet trying to push my slippers
under the bed …

It was soundless that I heard the tree
sobbing about losing its leafy hair …

It was so still that
I finally fell
into a deep, dream-filled sleep …

Charlotte Alderson (11)
Beeford CE (VC) Primary School, Beeford

A Poem To Be Spoken Silently

(Inspired by 'A Poem to be Spoken Silently' by Pie Corbett)

It was so silent I heard
the carpet shake off dust …

It was so quiet I heard
My hair growing
out of my head …

It was so peaceful I heard
the spiders
spinning silky webs …

It was so silent I heard
the table giggle
as the chairs tickled its legs …

It was so quiet I heard
my rubber duck
talk to the soap …

It was so calm I could hear
the friendly moon gossiping
one last time before he
said goodbye.

Liam Kelly (11)
Beeford CE (VC) Primary School, Beeford

A Poem To Be Spoken Silently

(Inspired by 'A Poem to be Spoken Silently' by Pie Corbett)

It was so calm that I heard
the stars playing and giggling
with each other …

It was so silent that I felt
my drawers aching
so full of clothes …

It was so quiet that I heard
the taps comparing
their shiny coats …

It was so peaceful I could hear
my friendly moon
gossiping one last time
before he said goodbye …

It was so quiet that I could hear
the pictures laughing
as the walls tickled them …

Thomas Gordge
Beeford CE (VC) Primary School, Beeford

A Poem To Be Spoken Silently

(Inspired by 'A Poem to be Spoken Silently' by Pie Corbett)

It was so silent I heard
the walls moaning
under the weight of the roof …

It was so still I could hear
the taps comparing
their shiny coats …

It was so silent I heard
the tiles tapping
as they swapped place in the bathroom
'I'll stay here, you go over there …'

It was so peaceful I heard
the friendly moon gossiping
one last time
before he said goodbye …

Zak Mayo
Beeford CE (VC) Primary School, Beeford

Christmas Pudding

Who ate the Christmas pudding?
It can't be Mum,
She is busy making dinner ...

It can't be Sister, she is happily playing
With her toys ...

It can't be Brother,
He's having a nap ...

It can't be Dad
He's working hard ...

So it must be the dog!
Well, that's what I think anyway!

Javi Rochelle (10)
Beeford CE (VC) Primary School, Beeford

Polar Bear

Polar bear
Seal hunter
Big carnivore
Seals are doomed
When he is around
Surprise or straight on
90% ends in a kill
It can almost out run anything
It definitely is a killer.

Gareth Harris (9)
Bilton Grange CP School, Harrogate

Cheetah

Prowling through the jungle,
Looking for its prey.
Hoping to feed itself
For another day.

With its dazzling spots
And extremely long tail.
It runs 1,000 times faster
Than your average snail.

It sprints up trees,
To find a hiding place.
It scares the birds,
Then carries on, on its chase.

With its huge gleaming teeth
And its jet-black eyes.
It could just be enough
To give you a surprise!

Chloe Marshall (10)
Bilton Grange CP School, Harrogate

Dog – Cinquain

Fluffy
Very rough feet
Soft fur and floppy ears
Long and short hair, scruffy and neat
Pink ears.

Nicola Williams (10)
Bilton Grange CP School, Harrogate

Winter

Wrap up warm
Warm and safe
Gales, hails,
All night long
Roasty fire
Rosy cheeks
Snowball fights
All day long
Sledges out
Across the field of white
Skaters on a frozen pond
Watching for ice breaks.
World of white all around
As night comes, fun has gone
Mr Frost is here to cover the white
With a glittering film
Silent and still.

Matthew Craig-Ramsden (9)
Bilton Grange CP School, Harrogate

Sirius Black – Cinquain

Betrayed
Good sorcerer
Never a killing man
Harry Potter's good Godfather
Not bad.

Chavy Mtawali (10)
Bilton Grange CP School, Harrogate

A Dog

His head he likes me to pat
He doesn't like the next-door neighbour's cat
He doesn't like the milkman, he's not a very big fan
And he barks all day at the postman's van
He loves to chew my dad's socks
But whenever someone comes to the door and knocks
He barks forever long
Until the visitor is gone
When he goes to the vets
He barks at other pets
He likes eating his food
He'll eat it all if he is in a good mood
He likes to be stroked
But he doesn't like to be poked
He will lick his paw
Till his tongue gets sore.

Roisin Swainston-Rainford (10)
Bilton Grange CP School, Harrogate

Earth – Haiku

Massive ball of life
Steadily turning around
Changing day and night.

Joseph Atkinson (9)
Bilton Grange CP School, Harrogate

The Touring Car Race

Cool ride,
Powerslide,
Windows smash,
Drivers thrash,
Kitted up,
Wanting cup,
So quick,
Killing the gearstick,
White knuckles,
Seatbelt buckled,
Too fast,
Racing past,
Speeding pace,
White face,
Gotta win the touring car race.

Ki-Ten Pat Lorridana-Atkinson (10)
Bilton Grange CP School, Harrogate

Penguin

Fast swimmer
Slow walker
A prey
Multicoloured
Food catcher
Likes cold
Flipper flapper.

Reece Campbell (9)
Bilton Grange CP School, Harrogate

Poetry Explorers — Yorkshire

Animals

Some are wide and some are small
Some are thin and some are tall.
Owls and bats come out at night,
Pumas and tigers give you a fright.
Cheetahs with their extremely long tails,
Slugs as slow as your average snail.
Foxes, leopards, panthers all,
Cannot beat the wolves' mighty call.
The grace of a butterfly,
The wisdom of an owl,
Could never live up to
The lion's growl.
Rodents, reptiles, amphibians, mammals,
Couldn't be anything apart from animals.

Phoebe Hanslow (10)
Bilton Grange CP School, Harrogate

My Guinea Pig

Knock at the door, she does a squeak,
But when I stroke her she falls asleep,
When she is stroked she smiles with glee
And she is very cuddly.
Her name is Lucky, isn't that cute?
And she is scared of the sound of the flute.
She has a sister called Fee,
And they will love each other forever, you'll see.

Lottie Willmore (9)
Bilton Grange CP School, Harrogate

Crocodile

Mr crocodile's teeth so sharp
Why are you so harsh?
Always on the prowl, eating here and there
Swimming in the swamp eating fish everywhere.
He snaps at any creature he eats,
Swimming fast or running on clawed foot
Very big in weight or in size
Really big, slimy and scaly and always on a rampage
People always lock them in cages.
A crocodile is a demon thing
They lurk below the water edge waiting for an unsuspecting prey
Then snaps those jaws of steal.

Kyle Wallace (10)
Bilton Grange CP School, Harrogate

Gymnastics

I love gymnastics, I think it's totally hip,
I get to run and jump and spring and flip.
When I go on the beam it feels like a dream,
When I mess up on vault, I know that it is all my fault.
And when we finish on the bars, we know that the gymnastics
                                                                      floor is ours!
I love my gymnastics class,
Our coach is Mrs Grasp.
We dress in a leotard so bright and pink,
And when we have a break, I get a big drink.

Amy Noble (10)
Bilton Grange CP School, Harrogate

Footwear

High heels to go out
Here and there, all about
Wellies to splash in mud
Slippers to wear cosy and good
Pumps easy to pack
Sandals to make a beach track
Trainers to run
Flip-flops to wear in the sun
And soft shoes are to dance
Riding boots so soft and light
What we wear must be just right.

Katalin Holstead (10)
Bilton Grange CP School, Harrogate

Dogs

Loud barking at night,
When it is not bright.
Scaring cats,
Chasing rats.
Running like a car,
But not so far.
In the kennel in the house,
You're faster than a mouse.
Barking loud, barking quiet,
Some need to be on a diet.

Cameron Phillips (9)
Bilton Grange CP School, Harrogate

Dog

Lazy-bones
Feet-warmer
Sock-snatcher
Toe-licker
Treat-muncher
Stick-fetcher
Ball-lover
Fluffy-fur.

Lewis Parker (10)
Bilton Grange CP School, Harrogate

Siberian Tiger

Prowling tiger burning bright
In the middle of the night
With your teeth so very sharp
And you always run so fast
With your claws that crush all bones
Everyone's scared and you should know
He's a Siberian tiger so get out of the way
Or you will never be seen another day.

Catherine Greenham (9)
Bilton Grange CP School, Harrogate

Poetry Explorers – Yorkshire

Moving On!

It gnaws at the back of my head all night.
Knocking the breath out of me in the morning.
My heart is racing fast, trying to break out of my chest.

Although I have long prepared for this day,
It still seems to wind me at the thought.

My legs feel numb as I walk down slowly to the kitchen.
All different emotions overwhelm me as I take the last bite of cereal
and head for the door.

With fumbling fingers I do up my shoelaces and
shrug on my new blazer,
I kiss my mother on the cheek and she wishes me good luck.

I feel scared and lonely as I get a ticket for the bus.
Nerves and excitement have a raging battle
deep in the pit of my stomach.
Making me feel sick,
I try to convince myself I'm excited.

It is working for a white, till I can see a tall building looking overhead.
My nerves immediately swallow me up in a dark shadow, as all the
children walk past me in the yard.

I feel dizzy as I walk in, I can feel the blood drain from my face as
I look around.

But then I see a young girl looking lost, confused and out of place,
just like me.
I ask her name and my heart does a triple flip.
She smiles with obvious appreciation and relief at my feeble attempt
to be friendly.

I think I might fly, when we walk into school hand in hand as best
friends.

Ellie Croft (11)
Cawood CE (VA) Primary School, Selby

My Bad Box

(Based on 'Magic Box' by Kit Wright)

I will put in my box ...
An ear-piercing cry,
Thick blood oozing from a cut,
Nerves that always target me.

I will put in my box ...
My terrifying nightmares,
A colourless world,
An electric crack of lightning.

I will put in my box ...
People who think the only person in the world is them,
The chilly breeze biting away at me,
Global warming that could make the species of the Earth extinct.

I will put in my box ...
Bullying that bullies think is OK,
Murderers and thieves,
Kidnappers and knife crimes.

My box is fashioned from teardrops,
Stained with blood,
And prison to all bad memories.

I shall burn my box,
And bury the ashes,
Hoping that no one will set the demon free.

Ellen Dethridge (10)
Cawood CE (VA) Primary School, Selby

Poetry Explorers – Yorkshire

My Bad Box

(Based on 'Magic Box' by Kit Wright)

In my box I will put my nightmare that came true.
A school trip that takes you to Hell.
A ghostly whisper in the dark of night.

In my box I will put the feeling on a morning when I have to get up and go to school.
A quiver when I hear something bad.
Global warming destroying and taking over the world.

I will put in my box people downstairs in the pub, having loud conversations while I am trying to go to sleep.
Rich men being greedy, not giving the poor enough to live.
Bullies thinking that they have the right to ruin kids' education.

My box is made out of the highest point of Mount Everest with nightmares and mysteries locked up inside it.
I will bury my box in the hope that no one ever finds it …

Jacob Linley (11)
Cawood CE (VA) Primary School, Selby

The Magic Box

(Based on 'Magic Box' by Kit Wright)

I will put in my box, my last piece of luxurious chocolate with a centre of oozing caramel.

I will put in my box, the scent of roses lingering over the Earth's atmosphere, covering it with a luscious smell.

I will put in my box, the joy and happiness of children playing and their exhilarated laugh on their euphoric faces.

I will put in my box, the natural world crying out to me on a lovely summer's day.

My box is fashioned from the most expensive jewels money can buy. Its golden hinges are made from gold mined from the underground of Africa
And its lid is made from soft leopard skin.

I will treasure my box in the innermost place of my heart.

Luke Royle (10)
Cawood CE (VA) Primary School, Selby

Happiness

Happiness skips up to you when you are lonely.
Happiness is bright and breezy like a cold winter's morning.
Happiness jumps around putting a smile on everyone's face.
Happiness is yellow just like the sun.
Happiness is a baby's first smile.
That's what I call happiness.

Harriet McCowliff (11)
Cawood CE (VA) Primary School, Selby

Poetry Explorers – Yorkshire

Love Is A Fairground

Love is a fairground,
All the places to go.

Love is a roller coaster,
The ups, the downs,
The twirl arounds.

Love is a ghost train,
Scary at times.

Love is like dodgems,
The hits,
The misses.

Love is like the waltzer,
Dancing in harmony together.

Love is love.

Rosie Hutton (11)
Cawood CE (VA) Primary School, Selby

Fog

Fog is like a white ghost swiftly gliding through the sky trying to put her cold touch on our spring mornings.

She will visit you from time to time greeting you with a delicate kiss.

She stands in front of you hiding the trees and buildings then will cover you with her blanket.

But by break of the next day she will have silently disappeared.

Sam Cheetham (10)
Cawood CE (VA) Primary School, Selby

The Cat

The cat is a purring ball of fur.
It sleeps like a satiated lion,
Stirring only to survey its surroundings.
A hunter.
Like an eagle in the sky,
A shark in the sea,
Seeking and allowing no escape.
But friendship and love,
It needs.
Like a newborn baby needs its mother
To make it feel safe.
Purr, purr, purr
The cat is secure and content.

Lizzie Langdale (10)
Cawood CE (VA) Primary School, Selby

Tornado

He twisted and turned in an angry rage
He threw upturned cars and picked up roofs.
Palm trees fell upon a road.

Fragments of glass fell onto the grass
Like rain of a different kind.
And then it fell silent.
Silent as the snow on a winter's morning.

William Dennis (11)
Cawood CE (VA) Primary School, Selby

Rain

As I walk to school in the morning
I wish I was warm and cosy in bed
The wind howls like a scary wolf
I pull up my hood to cover my head.

As I get closer to school I think
It is such a pain that I have to see all
The teachers again and again.

I walk in through the door
It's like walking into the summer
As I leave the cold and dark behind.

Eve Bray (10)
Cawood CE (VA) Primary School, Selby

My Bedroom

I like to see my bed staring at me as I enter the room,
It moves towards me on all four legs,
My chair sits there in the corner,
It smiles at me in the night and hugs me in the morning,
I like to see my mirror stare at me as I walk in the room,
Some days it's happy and other days it's sad,
When I am feeling pretty it grins at me like a Cheshire cat,
My chest of drawers has its mouth hanging open,
Clothes dribble out like spilt food,
It stands in the corner, still and dark.

Ellie Edwards (11)
Cawood CE (VA) Primary School, Selby

Friendship

Friendship is a soft gentle hand,
Friendship is a warm welcoming smile,
Friendship is the laughs at the park,
Friendship is that gentle face,
Friendship is the hide-and-seek fun,
Friendship is a kind voice of encouragement,
Friendship is skipping with friends.

Emma Howie (10)
Cawood CE (VA) Primary School, Selby

The Big Bang

Bang! Crash! Smash! Whirl!
Crying out, the big bang comes alive.
An amazing atomic bang!
Like a super serpent flying through the universe.
Whiz, whoosh, race, chase, crash, smash!
The big bang!
World's end or world's beginning?
Apocalypse of Eden's garden
Creeping, crawling, down miles of deep, dark tunnel!
600,000,000 bangs a second,
Atoms and protons clashing together!
At last
… The *big* bang!

Nathan Jeffs (9)
High Bentham CP School, High Bentham

Poetry Explorers – Yorkshire

Magic Of The Brain

Such a soft fur I felt.
Black fur as black as pitch-black darkness,
As soft as floating clouds in the sunny bright sky,
I feel all warm and joyful,
Such a soft fur I felt.

Such a sound I heard,
My friends laughing and cheering,
I felt all warm inside as their giggles
filled the air with joy,
Such a sound I heard

And such a sight I saw,
My friends smiling,
Their faces drowned in twinkly sparkles
as their mouths covered their face with their smile,
Such a sight I saw.

Such a taste I tasted,
Creamy chocolate ice cream,
It melted in my mouth and big loud crunches
were heard as I bit into the toppings on top,
Such a taste I tasted.

Rosie Fletcher (10)
High Bentham CP School, High Bentham

The Big Bang!

Bang!
One of the biggest experiments of our time has started,
The mighty monster rears and opens its gigantic jaws,
As the miniscule atoms are placed inside,
Apocalypse or Eden nursery?
We're all waiting breathlessly,
Bang!
Crash!
Whizz!
Zoom!
Smash!
Whoosh!
The monster wakes up slowly, slowly,
And lets its tough tongue push the atoms down his throat,
And through his monstrous body,
At -217.3 degrees it's like the South Pole,
The atoms whizz along like a flying bird,
They spread their wings and set off,
Until they meet at the end with a bang,
... The big bang!

Charlotte Green (10)
High Bentham CP School, High Bentham

Poetry Explorers – Yorkshire

Chocolate To Me

I love the pleasure of chocolate,
As it melts upon my tongue,
It dribbles all through my mouth,
And squishes around my gums,

I love the pleasure of chocolate,
It's smooth and very yummy,
It slips and slides all through my throat,
As it goes down to my tummy.

Amy Lawson (9)
High Bentham CP School, High Bentham

The Big Bang

In the centre of the Earth
in a metal pod
the atoms fight the protons
in their civil war
back-ups coming at a rate of 3 million a second.
Bang, crash, whizz
Suddenly an eerie silence
The end of the world?

William Jackson (10)
High Bentham CP School, High Bentham

Chocolate Poem

I love the pleasure of chocolate
As it melts upon my tongue
It dribbles through my mouth
And squishes around my gums
I love the pleasure of chocolate
It's smooth and chocolatey
But most of all I'd like to have it
For breakfast, lunch and tea!

Aimee Read (10)
High Bentham CP School, High Bentham

The Sea's Like A Peregrine Falcon

The sea is like a peregrine falcon chasing his prey.
He swoops and dives and scrapes the rocky cliffs
with his talons all day.
With his huge wings folded and his eyes on his prey
the giant bird crashes!
Onto the shore.
Cleaning his wings at his nest and the howl of the captured prey.

Calum Cochrane (9)
High Bentham CP School, High Bentham

Ears Hear

Crowds roar,
Drums boom,
Stars rock,
Fireworks zoom
Hips shake,
Guitars strum,
Kids hum: *Mm, mm.*

Lauren Atkinson (10)
High Bentham CP School, High Bentham

The Sea Is A Giant Dog

The sea is a giant dog, running up the shore
roaring and pounding together for evermore,
He rolls on the beach all day, with his tail high and his paws low.

The giant dog chases his tail and makes a whirlpool as he goes,
Licking his paws and putting his head between his legs,
He finally goes to sleep.

Bethany Jenkins (9)
High Bentham CP School, High Bentham

The Sea

The sea is a soaring eagle, gliding towards the shore
Golden and glistening he swoops onto the beach all day
With his claws at the ready and his eyes on his prey.
The giant bird flies over the stones and watches all below.

Elliott Andrews (10)
High Bentham CP School, High Bentham

Opposites

Sky
Vast, immense
Flying, looming, floating
Up, up and away, down, down below
Hopping, skipping, jumping
Grassy wet
Ground.

In
Sheltered, safe
Drawing, writing, thinking
Quiet and alone, busy and rushing
Shouting, ranting, waiting
Spacious, open
Out

Asleep
Warm, cosy
Dreaming, wondering, drifting
Silent and calm, up and about
Seeing, doing
Awake

Sad
Upset, worthless
Crying, whimpering, sobbing
Down in the dumps, over a rainbow
Smiling, grinning, hugging,
Bubbly, bright
Happy

Poetry Explorers – Yorkshire

Hot
Warm, toasty
Sunbathing, drinking, cooling
Having water fights, sipping hot chocolate
Curling, snuggling, sleeping
Freezing, shivering
Cold.

Ella Mortimer (11)
Menston Primary School, Menston

My Dream

In my dream, I dreamt
I was a bird
Soaring through the sky
Way up high

In my dream, I dreamt
I was a dog
Eating my bone
In my home

In my dream, I dreamt
I was a cat
In my bed
Resting my head

In my dream, I dreamt
I was a fish
Swimming in my bowl
And I found a hole.

Sophie Robinson (9)
Menston Primary School, Menston

Seaside

Ice creams as white as the clouds
In the bright clear sky.
The sea as blue as sapphires
Sparkling bright.

The golden sand shimmers
Like the queen's treasures.
The sweet smell of steamy hot dogs
Fill my nostrils.

Martha Whitaker (9)
Menston Primary School, Menston

Deep Under The Sea

I can hear the waves rushing
I can see the fish jumping,
Deep under the sea.

I can see the crabs scuttling,
I can hear the seaweed rustling,
Deep under the sea.

I can hear my breath bubbling,
I can see the mermaids swimming,
Deep under the sea.

I can see the coral reefs waving,
I can hear the dolphins screeching,
In my dreams!

Lucy Turner (10)
Menston Primary School, Menston

Poetry Explorers – Yorkshire

The 5 Senses Of Cheese

Cheese, cheese, mouldy cheese
How I like the smell of it
Cheese, cheese, squishy cheese
How I like the feel of it.

Porridge, porridge, manky porridge
How I hate the texture of it
Porridge, porridge, soggy porridge
How I hate the taste of it.

Cheese, cheese, spready cheese
Oh how soft and munchy
Cheese, cheese, crackers and cheese
Oh how I like my crackers crunchy.

Mushrooms, mushrooms, black and soft
I hate them in my Spag Bol!
Mushrooms, mushrooms, squishy mushrooms
I hate them like my sister's doll!

Cheese, cheese, melting cheese
I hear it bubbling on my toast
Cheese, cheese, yummy cheese
I like most cheese, except for goat.

Fish, fish, oily fish
Forget about (Omega 3)
Fish, fish, slimy fish
Come from the dirty sea.

Cheese, cheese, I see cheese
It's in my kitchen fridge
Cheese, cheese, scrumptious cheese
Edam, Gorgonzola, Cheddar and Red Leicester
I love all of it …

Bradley Brown (10)
Menston Primary School, Menston

Magical Horse

In a magical world,
There is one creature,
Some way out in wide open land
And there are grass and trees.

There are lots of creatures to choose,
But trying to find the animal you are trying to find,
Is somewhere beautiful and full of magic,
So you need to find it in a flick.

It can't be far,
Because it's somewhere near,
And it will come near you,
So don't be scared.

It can't be small,
They're too small to find,
My creature gallops and walks,
So it must be near.

Fine I'll tell you three more clues:
My creature's brown and,
Gallops a lot,
But not a pest.

Guess it please,
Fine I'll tell you,
My animal is a horse,
Galloping in the field.

To ride on a horse,
Is my kind of dream
To play and enjoy,
So peaceful it will seem.

Stacy Ramsey (10)
Menston Primary School, Menston

Poetry Explorers – Yorkshire

The Underwater World!

In the underwater world,
There are so many creatures.
Some way out to sea,
And some near sandy beaches.

There are lots to choose,
Of all these animals.
But definitely my favourite,
Are some fast swimming mammals.

It can't be a turtle,
They're too slow.
Sharks are a fish,
And too much of a foe.

It can't be a whale;
They dive too deep.
My type of creature,
Goes jump, spin and leap.

OK, three more clues,
My creature is grey.
Chatters quite a lot,
And loves to play.

Guessed it yet?
Fine I'll tell you.
My fave is a dolphin,
Swimming in the blue.

To swim with a dolphin,
Is my kind of dream.
To play and enjoy
So peaceful, it will seem.

Tom Luxton (10)
Menston Primary School, Menston

What Has Happened To Kitty?

(Based on 'What has happened to Lulu?' by Charles Causley)

What has happened to Kitty, Daddy?
What has happened to Kit?
There's nothing left but her red bowl and cushion
A place she liked to sit.

Why is her food untouched, Daddy?
Her milk is stale and sour
I've looked around the house, I've searched high and low
Now I wait for her hour by hour.

When will she come back home, Daddy?
Remember her silky fur
I like stroking her shiny coat
Please say you remember her.

Why is her bed so cold, Daddy?
No footprints on the floor
Why are there no feathers around the house?
There is no smell any more.

Why has she disappeared, Daddy?
Why has she disappeared?
I miss her going up to the fire
Where she sneered.

Can you hear that, Daddy?
The cat flap creeping open
And hear that silent purr
Kitty!

Millie Baxter (9)
Menston Primary School, Menston

Poetry Explorers – Yorkshire

Monkeys

Monkeys in the trees
Swinging for their food.
Monkeys in the trees
Swinging for their food.

Monkeys in the rainforests
Losing their habitat.
Monkeys in the rainforest
Losing their habitat.

Monkeys in the zoos
Thinking they'd rather be free.
Monkeys in the zoos
Thinking they'd rather be free.

Monkeys in the trees
With their babies cuddled up.
Monkeys in the trees
With their babies cuddled up.

Monkeys in the rainforest
Fighting for survival.
Monkeys in the rainforest
Fighting for survival.

Monkeys in the zoos
Being caught first.
Monkeys in the zoos
Being caught first.

Gemma Wright (9)
Menston Primary School, Menston

Hogan My New Puppy

We are all excited
A new puppy at home
What fun it will be
Got the lead and a bone

Gosh his teeth are sharp
He jumps and nips
Pulling at my trousers
All my comics he rips

I keep standing in his puddles
He's whining and barking at night
He always wants to sit on my knee
He chews everything in sight

It's harder than I thought
Waiting outside in the rain
For my puppy to be clean
Nothing will ever be the same

Mum said we should wait
A puppy is very hard work
I promised I'd look after it
I think I've been a berk!

Although he's really naughty
Watching him all the time
I still love him lots and
I can't believe he's mine.

Robbie Hirst (9)
Menston Primary School, Menston

Swimming Along With Me

The dolphin glides along the sea,
Swimming along with me.
Bobbing up and down,
Never wearing a frown.
Swimming along with me.

Glistening in the moonlight breeze,
Swimming along with me.
Having fun in the light of the moon,
The sun coming up soon.
Swimming along with me.

Eating its afternoon tea,
Swimming along with me.
Shining a brightly blue,
Calling for a kindly you.
Swimming along with me.

Sings, does he,
Swimming along with me.
Echoing through the big, wide ocean,
Moving in a swift motion.
Swimming along with me.

Swimming along,
Swimming along,
Swimming … along … with … me!

Kezia Finch (9)
Menston Primary School, Menston

Hullabaloo

I raised a great hullabaloo
When I found out it wasn't true
Gran's not dead
She's asleep in bed!

She was reading
Now she's dreaming
Dad's so amazed
He asked for a raise.

Now he's been fired
And then rehired
We are so rich
I don't live in a ditch.

I've got a new dog
And his name is Rog
He's got a toy
That brings him joy.

My mum's a cook
And she's written a book
So much food
It's radical dude!

Sam Simons (10)
Menston Primary School, Menston

If I Were A Dragon

If I were a dragon,
I would fly to the top of Earth,
I could bathe in the sea,
If I were a dragon.

If I were a dragon,
I could destroy what I like,
I would breathe fire,
If I were a dragon.

If I were a dragon,
I would live in a cave,
And guard my treasure,
If I were a dragon.

If I were a dragon,
I would be nearly invincible,
Arrows would bounce off me,
If I were a dragon.

If I were a dragon
You could smell my fiery breath,
You would see flames drifting out of my mouth,
If I were a dragon.

Robbie Sandground (9)
Menston Primary School, Menston

Snow

The playground icy
Menston Primary School was closed
The children happy

I had two cold hands
I put on two left wellies
It felt so weird

I had snowball fights
At the park with my best friends
And made a snowman

Sledging down a hill
Hurting my knees all the way
Views are beautiful

I had wet clothes on
All the time when I played
Came home very cold

I had hot chocolate
Sitting in front of fire
Keeping nice and warm.

Tom Palmer (10)
Menston Primary School, Menston

Poetry Explorers – Yorkshire

My Pets

I have a fish,
That swims all day.
Also a dog.
That likes to play.
I have a cat.
That's small and cute.
Also an owl.
That likes to hoot.
I have a hamster.
That likes its wheel.
Also a pig.
That munches its meal.
I have a guinea pig.
That loves to sleep.
Also a frog.
That likes to leap.
I have a hedgehog.
That always goes to the vets
These are all my pets!

Katie-Rose Mortimer (9)
Menston Primary School, Menston

Trapped – Haiku

I look at the birds
Gliding through the starlit sky
And wish I could fly.

Jamie Jerome (9)
Menston Primary School, Menston

What Has Happened To Jenny?
(Based on 'What has happened to Lulu?' by Charles Causley)

What has happened to Jenny, Auntie?
What has happened to Jen?
The sand in her cage lying so still
Where she had her den.

Where is my lovely lizard, Auntie?
Do you know where she is?
L'il Jenny is lost,
I almost called her Liz.

Her warm bed is cold now
Where could she be?
Have you any idea where she is?
Remember when she would climb on my knee?

Last night I had a dream
That she was there in front of me.
What has happened to Jenny, Auntie?
Where on Earth is she?

Anna Middleton (9)
Menston Primary School, Menston

Snow

S ee the wonderful white stuff land
N owhere to go but on the ground
O h everybody loves the snow, but
W hy does it have to melt and go?

Ellie Benn (10)
Menston Primary School, Menston

Poetry Explorers – Yorkshire

What Has Happened To Bo-Bo?
(Based on 'What has happened to Lulu?' by Charles Causley)

What has happened to Bo-Bo, Mother?
What has happened to Bo?
There is nothing left but her string ball Mother
The one she used to show.

I have looked under the sofa Mother
I have searched high and low
Where has she gone Mother?
Where did she go?

Do you know where she has gone Mother?
Is she in the house?
Tell me Mother, tell me
Because I can smell a mouse.

Where is Bo-Bo Mother?
Where is Bo-Bo the cat?
Is she nearby Mother?
Or is she under the doormat?

Abigail Spencer (9)
Menston Primary School, Menston

Snow

S ledges flying really high
N ow it's time to start the fun
O h no it's time to go
W ow that was the best race ever!

Maria Sage (7)
Menston Primary School, Menston

The Winter Snow

The winter snow
Covers the land like a pure white blanket
The black ice makes all the cars
Slip and crash into the deep walls.

The winter snow
Is as thick as a cloud
Icicles hang from walls
Like sharp swords going for enemies.

The winter snow
Falls to the ground like candyfloss
It melts
As soon as it hits the floor.

The winter snow
Crunches when you step on it
Like leaves being trodden on
That have fallen from trees.

Phoebe Walker (8)
Menston Primary School, Menston

Space Acrostic Poem

S tars twinkling in the night
P eople wondering what it's like to be in space
A nimals sent up in space
C louds of gases form above the Earth
E arth orbiting the sun.

Jack Hargreaves (10)
Menston Primary School, Menston

Poetry Explorers – Yorkshire

I'm Not Telling You

I'm not telling you my secret
My secret is secret to me.
And if I tell you my secret
It will not be a secret to me.

I'm not telling you where I live
Where I live is a secret to me.
And if I tell you where I live
It will not be a secret to me.

I'm not telling you all my friends
All my friends are a secret to me.
And if I tell you all my friends
They will not be a secret to me.

I like to keep secrets
Because secrets stay with me,
So if I tell anyone my secrets
They will not be a secret to me.

Alice Jackson (8)
Menston Primary School, Menston

Sheep

S ilent when being led through pastures,
H ighlands the home of many,
E verlasting grass chewing,
E ternal sitting in a field,
P astures where small newborn lambs lie down.

Jonathan Britton (10)
Menston Primary School, Menston

The Cup Winners Cup

Emily supports Chelsea
Saw the team in blue and white
She was glad the score was three nil
Finally won the Premier League

Confidently beat Stoke
Frank Lampard scored the winning goal
Everyone cheered and shouted
Chelsea had the victory

Louder and louder she screamed
Emily could see the cup
Gleaming in the captain's hands
Holding tight, the special cup.

In the end they went home happy
Having won the big bad fight
Seeing family and friends
They had fun celebrating.

Aimee Palmer (10)
Menston Primary School, Menston

A Nice Place

W onderful place to live your life
O pen space ready to be played on
R ed lava pouring out of the ground
L ovely huge trees that give us oxygen
D elicious fresh fruit that is wonderful and ripe.

James Hill (8)
Menston Primary School, Menston

Poetry Explorers – Yorkshire

The Sweet Shop

Night-time, the shop is fast asleep
The wind whistles through the door
The jelly babies are tucked up in bed by now
In their small sugar blankets all cosy and warm
The smell of sugar and candyfloss waft around the dark room

The clock ticks hour by hour
Tick tick, *ting!* The clock strikes twelve
'Wake up you lazy sweets, it's midnight! Party time!'
They yawn and make a fuss then slip on their dance shoes!
The Smartie is the first up to boogie then the Jelly Tot!

Time goes by, they all get very hot
The chocolate is now gooey
And is all over the shop's new, bright, shiny till's screen
They've had enough for one night they think! Not again!
Clear the shop up and to bed before it turns two!

Goodnight!

Grace Malir (10)
Menston Primary School, Menston

Fruit

F ruit is very good for you,
R ipe fruit all summertime,
U se apples for apple crumble,
I love lots of fruits, especially bananas,
T hanks to God for all of this.

Joe Westwood (9)
Menston Primary School, Menston

That Cat

Look next-door, it's that cat
Rushing through the hedge,
There it is once again
Sitting on the window ledge.

It can't catch a cold
Let alone a mouse,
There it is once again
Let it in the house!

See it looking for its food
Take a look, a jumping flea!
There it is once again
Spying on its enemy.

Look next-door, it's that cat
Rushing through the hedge,
There it is once again
Sitting on the window ledge.

Rory Haggart (11)
Menston Primary School, Menston

Weather

Thunder, thunder, thunder.
Rain, rain, rain.
The sun comes out.
The rain goes away.
We all come out and play.

Mary Slack (10)
Menston Primary School, Menston

Poetry Explorers – Yorkshire

Sporting Stories Poem

Sprinting down the rugby pitch
Wilkinson kicked the ball
Pieterson ran onto it
And he charged at them all

Schumacher was on the grid
Button was beside him
Round the first bend Button crashed
Both men wanted to win

Andy Murray served the ace
Nadal could not take it
He became so very mad
And threw down his racket

Gerrard stood up to the ball,
Kicked it with all his might
It hit a fan in the head
It was a funny sight.

Benjamin Lulham-Robinson (10)
Menston Primary School, Menston

My Hamster

My hamster is small, furry and sweet.
Every now and again he likes a treat.
He likes a lot of different things to eat.
Especially fruit and seeds but definitely not meat.
My hamster is funny and sweet.

Sophie Benn (8)
Menston Primary School, Menston

My Snow Poem

Today, a snow day
Can it be the best time, now?
Can we ever tell?

Sledging, ice skating,
Are so common at this time
Never forgotten.

So many snowmen
Always looking so happy
But cold, on snow days.

Hats keep our heads warm
And scarves are useful today
For today it's cold.

All happy today
For today is a snow day
A happy, snow day.

Jacob Knowland (10)
Menston Primary School, Menston

Sharks

S harks are very tough
H ave a very big fin
A nd they swim
R ough and very dangerous
K ill everything in sight.

David Bulcock (9)
Menston Primary School, Menston

Stop!

'Stop! Stop!' I cried
That's how it all began
But all they heard was *roar!*
So of course I tried to run.

'Stop! Stop!' I cried
When I found my strength again
I found it was no use
For I was locked up in a pen.

'Stop! Stop!' I cried
As they trained me hard
I could hardly sleep at all
As I gazed at the rotten bars.

So here I am now
Stop is no use anymore
One person can do so much harm.

Milly Brown (10)
Menston Primary School, Menston

Winter

W ind howling.
I ndoor glow.
N ight drawing quickly.
T eddy hugging tight.
E erie silence all night.
R eady for morning, night night.

Joe Woollin (8)
Menston Primary School, Menston

Oh Pony

Oh pony, oh pony
Where have you gone?
I cannot see you
Anywhere, anywhere.
I looked, looked everywhere.
I cannot see you
Anywhere, anywhere.
I have looked in the stable everywhere
Looked in the field everywhere
Been down the road everywhere
Oh pony, oh pony
Please come home.
Oh pony, oh pony
I have found you
Oh pony, oh pony
Thank you for coming home.

Alessandra Ricci (8)
Menston Primary School, Menston

Winter

Winter, winter
When will it stop?
We've kept the dog in, it's barking too much

Winter, winter
When will it stop?
We want to go out but it's snowing too much.

Harry Watson (7)
Menston Primary School, Menston

Poetry Explorers – Yorkshire

Maddy The Horse

Neigh, neigh, neigh
Says Maddy's mouth
In the riding ring
Jumping over jumps
Whilst her rider's bouncing up and down

'Stop, stop, stop!'
The teacher yells
'That's enough today'
'Stop,' says the rider to her horse,
'We'll have to start again tomorrow.'

Chomp, chomp, chomp
Chomps Maddy
Eating in her stall
Crunching a little carrot
Oh what a good horse you are.

Lucy Campbell (9)
Menston Primary School, Menston

Balloons – Haiku

Balloons floating by,
Children having fun with them,
Children jumping high.

Balloons floating by
Rainbow colours everywhere,
Children loving them.

Toby Berry (10)
Menston Primary School, Menston

Manchester United

M anchester have the ball
A nderson has a fall
N emanja Vidic takes the ball off Anderson
C heeky Van der Sar is up field
H ear the roar of the fans
E veryone cheers so loud
S o loud the ground shakes
T ops are flung into the crowd
E nd of match Manchester win.
R ooney hugs Ronaldo

U nder the stands are the dressing rooms
N ani has gone already
I t might be because he didn't score
T oast is served in the dressing room
E nd of the day, the players have gone
D ying to see their families.

Nathan Twigg (9)
Menston Primary School, Menston

Seaside

S easide memories, captured in time,
E ndless views of the silky sand,
A ll seashells lie there, frozen in time,
S and all dry away from the waves,
I nside the turquoise sea, fish swerve,
D omes, sandy, cover the beach,
E very person passing by, stops to take a photograph.

Holly Margerrison (11)
Menston Primary School, Menston

A Long Day's Work

Through the curtains the light shines in,
Wake up in the morning show no grin,
See your teacher in the playground,
Walk in calmly without a sound.

The first lesson today is mathematics,
Do it well and don't get static,
After that it's yummy dinner,
Eat it quick you'll get out sooner.

Never miss your after school clubs,
The whole place is full of thugs,
Getting dark, time for bed,
Try to rest your sleepy head.

All day you've tried your best,
Now it's time for a great long rest!

Benedict Lane (10)
Menston Primary School, Menston

My Cat

My cat is a
Food-eater
Dog-hater
Person-lover
Water-drinker
Face-cleaner
And a *perfect pet!*

Francis Westhead (8)
Menston Primary School, Menston

Football Is Cool

I play it at school
I play at the park
My friend plays it too.
My favourite team is Man U
But they don't wear blue
Their colour is red
What colour are you?
They score lots of goals
In-between the poles
When Man U score
The ball really rolls
The players look good on the pitch
I think it's because they are rich.
The crowd cheer with excitement
Hope they don't get a stitch.

Jonathan Lupton (10)
Menston Primary School, Menston

Gangster Rap

Bang, bang, bang
It's a gangster's gun
A guy was killed in a hit 'n' run

Walking on the street, there goes me
I see a guy doing a robbery
I call the cops
They arrive in bullet-proof tops.

Ashley Gomersall (10)
Menston Primary School, Menston

Where Am I?

The children walk in through the old wooden door,
Wiping their feet on the carpet floor.
Hang up their coats on the rusty metal pegs,
Dropping things on their feet and scratching their legs.
Fidgeting around on the plastic chairs,
Girls playing and fiddling with their hair.
Trying to do their best - finishing off their work,
They all start to talk and the adult goes berserk!

It's time to go outside and play,
This is probably the best part of the day.
Skip, run and walk around,
Shout and scream, make your sound.

Where am I?
I am in school, I am in Menston Primary School.

Charlotte Borwell (11)
Menston Primary School, Menston

Flowers

F lowers are beautiful
L ovely and colourful
O n the windowsill
W ind brushing past the flowers
E very flower has a different colour
R ain helps them grow
S un shines on the flowers.

Holly Ramsey (9)
Menston Primary School, Menston

Winter Snowman

My snowman is white
With a bright big orange nose
It has black small icy eyes
With four brilliant buttons
Sitting cosy on the snowman

My snowman is fun
With his big emerald green hat
And his bright stick small thin arms
Dissolving into the frost
Standing like a scarecrow.

My snowman has gone
The snowman, it has melted
How awful to say it's gone
My snowman has gone once again.

Bradley Burrows (9)
Menston Primary School, Menston

Acrostic

P atrick is his name
A dapted to talk is he
T hick as he is, his home is made of sand
R ock on Conch Street is his house
I diotic and stupid, he has a small brain
C onfused and dim
K ind to SpongeBob, Squidward and Sandy.

Robert Westwood (10)
Menston Primary School, Menston

Poetry Explorers – Yorkshire

Family

Family
Evening meals
Argue, discussion, talks,
Trips to see cousins, fathers and mothers
Hugging, kissing, sitting on laps
Getting together
Love.

Friends
Lots of fun
Walking, talking, smiling
Play with them, or fight with them
Running, shouting, frowning
Ignoring them
Enemies.

Isabelle Hill (11)
Menston Primary School, Menston

Snowman

S now is wonderful for playing with and fun
N earby park is good for fun
O ut in the snow playing with the snow
W ow it's a big snowman for playing with the snow
M y oh my the snow is deep
A ll the snow, white and cold
N ow I have to go back to school.

Tom Kirkham (8)
Menston Primary School, Menston

What Has Happened To Daisy?
(Based on 'What has happened to Lulu?' by Charles Causley)

What has happened to Daisy, Mother?
What has happened to Dais?
There's nothing left but her field full of grass
A place where she used to graze.

Why is her food untouched, Mother?
Her oats so stale and dry
I have searched the whole yard and the fields
Remember the way she used to lie?

Listen Mother, *clip-clop, clip-clop*
Hear that very joyous sound
It's her, Mother! I can hear her neigh
Daisy!

Eleanor Freeman (10)
Menston Primary School, Menston

Dragons

Fire-breather
Crop-killer
Scale-waver
Roar-echoer
Treasure-lover
Fast-flyer
Claw-clinger
The ultimate killing machine.

Tommy Hinchliff (10)
Menston Primary School, Menston

Winter

Wrap up warm, winter's on the way,
With blanket-like snow and slippery ice.

Wrap up warm, winter's on the way,
With cold fingers and freezing toes.

Wrap up warm, winter's on the way,
With flying snowballs and sledging.

Wrap up warm, winter's on the way,
With woolly hats, gloves and thick coats.

Wrap up warm, winter's on the way,
With hot chocolate and buttery toast.

Wrap up warm, winter's on the way,
With happiness and laughter every day.

Elizabeth Westhead (10)
Menston Primary School, Menston

Winter

Snow
Icicles hanging
Snow falling rapidly
Pine trees blowing loudly
Fires burning brightly
Children playing
Snow.

Erin Shaw (7)
Menston Primary School, Menston

A Week With My Brother

My brother's name is Ben,
He's just over ten,
We play rugby together on Sundays,
Back to boring school on Monday,
Tuesday Ben does tennis,
He's a little menace,
Wednesday we go to Cubs,
The place is full of thugs,
Thursday I do football,
Ben has friends to call,
Friday is a day of rest,
Because all week we've done our best,
Saturday is sport again,
Cubs' football is our game.

Seb Lane (8)
Menston Primary School, Menston

Sound And Silence

Sound
Merry, loud
Rushing, hurrying, booming
Noise around us, peace within us
Soothing, silencing, quieting
Soft, soundless
Silence.

Hazel Bate (11)
Menston Primary School, Menston

Poetry Explorers – Yorkshire

Winter

The wind blows through the frozen trees
You can hear the icicles clattering and shattering
Snowmen are built in every garden
The snow goes and the ice hardens.

The snowflakes fall from the sky
I climb the tree way up high
Snow slowly gliding down
Cars slip on the black ice rapidly
Children playing happily.

Snow on the rooftops
Icicles hanging from pipes
See the ice clear and white
Children throwing snowballs.

Rebecca Clarke (8)
Menston Primary School, Menston

I Have A Dream

I have a dream to dance.
When I hear the music my feet just want to prance.
Pulling on my dancing shoes
I love to do funky moves.

Working hard to improve.
Always gets me in the groove.
Tap, jazz, modern too,
This is what I love to do.

Ellie Myers (10)
Menston Primary School, Menston

Snow

In the winter's snow
We play amongst the snowmen
Laughing in the park

With the frozen ice
We slip and fall on the ice
We can hurt ourselves

Throwing snow is great
But don't throw snow at the face
Snow is wonderful

Snow is fantastic
Don't waste the snow while it's here
It's one week a year.

James Turland (10)
Menston Primary School, Menston

Fireworks

F ireworks are beautiful in the night sky.
I think it looks like an orchard of flowers.
R ising into the sky go Screamers.
E xploding fireworks all different colours.
'W ow! They're wonderful,' people shout and cheer.
O rchards of flowers in the sky, oh what a sight.
R ich ruby reds, mouth-watering maroons.
K ing of them all is the mighty rocket.
S ee them all on Bonfire Night.

Olivia Deacon (8)
Menston Primary School, Menston

Winter's Day

When I wake up in the morning,
Everything is white with snow,
The winter air is cold and bitter,
I'll have fun today, I know.

Sliding down the hills on sledges,
I scream with laughter all the way,
Icy snowflakes fall around me,
How I love to laugh and play.

When the sun sets in the sky,
My toes and nose are cold and numb,
I am tired and very hungry,
I knew today would be such fun.

James Myers (9)
Menston Primary School, Menston

Football

Football is a very great sport
You can even play it indoors
It gives you time to show off your skill
Even in a practice drill

Football is cool
Football is cool
Give this sport a very good go
Then you'll have the choice to say yes or no.

Miles Charlesworth (9)
Menston Primary School, Menston

My Sweet Cat

She is very cute
I adore her shiny coat
And her so small paws
I really love her soft purr

Her face is so warm
Her eyes shine in the moonlight
Her small paws are cute
Her fur is a shiny white

She walks so lovely
Her best feature is her fur
I love my cute cat
I will never forget her.

Stanley Fleming (9)
Menston Primary School, Menston

The Snowman

The snow fell all through the night
Laying a blanket crisp and white
School closed all day
I go out in the garden and play.

I build a snowman with coal for eyes
Under the icy skies
He stays all day and night long
But when the sun shone he was gone.

Max McNeil (9)
Menston Primary School, Menston

I Love Football

Football is ace
I get in a good space
I chase the ball
I shoot it in the net

I play it in the mud
When the weather is good
I shake hands when
The match is over.

I love to play
All of the day
My football boots
Give me excellent grip.

Harriet Jackson (10)
Menston Primary School, Menston

Dog

Dog
Noisy, energetic
Running, chasing, jumping
Human lover, dog hater
Sleeping, eating, sneaking
Quiet, hunter
Cat.

Oliver Gibbs (10)
Menston Primary School, Menston

Car

We drive on the track
Drift past the corner
Rev up the engine
And off we go.

Fill up with petrol
Accelerate out
Speed on the long straight
Pull the handbrake.

When we have finished
Drive slowly back home
Park on the driveway
Rest for the night.

Oliver Mordey (9)
Menston Primary School, Menston

Sea

Sea
Bottomless, rippling
Swimming, diving, jumping
All around us, right below us
Running, walking, hiking
Rocky, motionless
Land.

Phoebe Connor (10)
Menston Primary School, Menston

My Cat

Cats, cats, my cat naps
In front of the fire
With me in bed
Oh I do admire.

Cats, cats, play with me
With their blue toys
My cat goes outside
Comes in making a noise.

Cats, cats make me laugh
Drink out of my tea cups
Rolling out the wool
Fall into bathtubs.

Georgia Forder (9)
Menston Primary School, Menston

Hamster

H appy time with my hamster
A fantastic friend
M e and my hamster
S tay with me
T oday I will laugh
E mily loves hamsters
R eady for hamster time!

Emily Lloyd (9)
Menston Primary School, Menston

My Dog Honey

She is beautiful
Her lovely coat is bright golden
She is very cute
No, she will never get sold!

She can't quite bark yet
She likes to bite my own foot
She's playing of course
She is a brilliant mutt.

Her paws are very big
She trips around the huge house
Her eyes are shiny
She is not scared of that old mouse.

Thomas Jackson (10)
Menston Primary School, Menston

Night And Day

Night
Dark, soundless
Sleeping, snoring, dreaming
The darkness is over, the light begins
Running, sweating, exhausting
Bright, colourful
Day.

Joseph Tindall (11)
Menston Primary School, Menston

Harvest Comes, Harvest Goes

Harvest brings the golden corn
Harvest brings the scattering of seeds
Farmers grow veg and wheat
Healthy and scrumptious that we will eat

Harvest brings the birds singing
Harvest brings sugar canes dropping
Bringing rain for the plants
Farmers ploughing all the fields

Harvest brings gigantic golden haystacks
Harvest brings fantastic food and drink
Then comes the church bells ringing
Happy harvest we are singing.

Callum Clarke (8)
Menston Primary School, Menston

What's A Friend?

F riends help you,
R un life with you if you're sad.
I 'm never happy without friends.
E at the sadness away from you.
N ext to your side all the time.
D rain all the sadness away from you.
S adness is never with you.

Charlie Kinsman (8)
Menston Primary School, Menston

If I Could Breathe Fire

If I could breathe fire
I would blow icicles off my dad's tyre.
If I had wings
I would fly up to the shimmering sun.

If I could run
I would enter a race and run as fast as a cheetah.
If I had four arms
I would hang from a tree all day.

If I could answer any question
I would play The Weakest Link!
If I had five eyes
I would be a security guard.

Hugh Berry (9)
Menston Primary School, Menston

Earth And Sky

Sky
Orange-peaceful
Gliding, flying, swifting
Rising above us, descending below us
Conquering, rushing, screeching
Noisy, revolting
Land.

Josh Hargreaves (10)
Menston Primary School, Menston

Owl

Perched on an old oak branch
Staring into the night
Watching the time go by
When it is not light.

Feeding chicks constantly
Nocturnal am I
My favourite hobby
Is to fly high.

Dark brown, grey, black or white
Young, old, big eyes, small
I am the oldest and
Wisest of them all.

Oliver Haggart (9)
Menston Primary School, Menston

Sadness

S mile, nowhere around her
A bbey her friend is being mean
D ay has just started horrible
N obody is talking to her
E verybody is ignoring her
S ad face as she cries
S unday morning is not perfect.

Ruby Richmond (9)
Menston Primary School, Menston

If I Were A Bee

If I were a bee
I would touch the sky
I would buzz all day
If I were a bee.

If I were a bee
I would pollinate the flowers
I would zoom through the sky
If I were a bee.

If I were a bee
I would make the honey
I would help the hive
If I were a bee.

Alfie Tennant (9)
Menston Primary School, Menston

Africa

Africa
Hot, dry
Sightseeing, climbing
Savannah all around us
Sledging, sliding, slipping
Icy, wet
Arctic.

Jack Smith (11)
Menston Primary School, Menston

The Cup Winners Cup

Mark supports Leeds United
Saw the team, in blue and white
He was glad they scored lots of goals
They finally won the league!

They won the gleaming cup
Louder people screamed
They are in the Championship
After a 3-1 victory.

Confidently beat Carlisle
The captain had thrown the ball
Mark had caught it in excitement
He had got it all.

Mark Wharrier (10)
Menston Primary School, Menston

The Family

F un-loving father
A nnoying sisters
M ud-hating mum
I ntelligent aunties and uncles
L oving grandparents
Y es I have brilliant friends as well!

Harry Myers (10)
Menston Primary School, Menston

Donkey Poem

Mine is the Eeyore
Tied up on a rope
Donkey rides I do
It's hard to cope

Me, starved if I don't
I hate my whole life
I wish I was dead
Help, I want the knife

Please give me some food
I will go on strike
So let me go please
I will eat his trike.

Harry Cooper (10)
Menston Primary School, Menston

Rabbit

R unning in the field like
A person in the Olympics
B ouncing around like a
B aseball player winning, we are talking about
I nspiration of a rabbit
T hey always jump up to you.

Adam France (9)
Menston Primary School, Menston

Fantastic Earth

Earth, Earth
There's lots of things about Earth
Earth is shaped like a blue and green ball
Earth, Earth!

Earth, Earth
Earth is so wonderful
God made Earth
Yes He did!

Earth, Earth
Earth is the best
I live on Earth
It's the best.

Riyah Chhokar & Ella Sanderson (9)
Menston Primary School, Menston

Vikings

V iolent Vikings
I nterested in treasure.
K illing Saxons.
I n their longships.
N ow we dig up Viking things.
G oing over the sea in the ships.

Michaela Devlin (7)
Menston Primary School, Menston

Cats!

Some cats are fat
And some cats are thin
Some cats are greedy
And eat out of the bin!

My friend's cat is cute
My cat is shy
My cousin's cat is cheeky
And can lift its paw to say hi!

There's a very spooky cat
That lives down my street
Miaow, miaow, miaow
That cat I have to meet!

Léona McLoughlin (9)
Menston Primary School, Menston

Spider

S ome are scary, some are not
P lacing webs wherever they trot
I f they only catch small bugs
D are they will to find some slugs
E very spider is scary to someone
R ear back from them or you'll become one.

Dhugal Sandground (7)
Menston Primary School, Menston

Poetry Explorers – Yorkshire

What Has Happened To Daisy?
(Based on 'What has happened to Lulu?' by Charles Causley)

What has happened to Daisy, Mum?
What has happened to Dais?
There's nothing left in the barn, Mum
Where she used to laze.

What has happened to Daisy, Mum?
Has Dad taken her?
Maybe to the auction mother
To shave Daisy's fur.

What has happened to Daisy, Mum?
What has happened to Dais?

Charley Smith (9)
Menston Primary School, Menston

Riyah The Mouse

Riyah, Riyah head of all mice.
The third smallest creature in the world.
The planet she lives on is the Earth.

Riyah, Riyah head of all mice.
Her best friend is Melissa the mouse.
Nothing, not even the king could tear them apart.

Riyah, Riyah head of all mice.
She has no swords, no guns, but ears big!
We all hail queen Riyah, you hail her too!

Melissa Redmond (9)
Menston Primary School, Menston

Horse

Horse, horse
Trotting very fast
Horse, horse
Faster than a deer.

Horse, horse
Flying through the air
Horse, horse
My horse is always there.

Horse, horse
After a day
Me and my horse are on our way.

Grace Slack (9)
Menston Primary School, Menston

Mum

My mum is fun and kind,
She is very pretty too,
And my mum has a great mind,
She always taught me sounds, my first was moo.

My mum helps me when I'm stuck,
And when I tread in muck,
My mum is always there to pick me straight back up,
I'm glad that I haven't run out of luck.

She's my mum and I love her.

Ellie Wilson (11)
Menston Primary School, Menston

Poetry Explorers – Yorkshire

Leeds United

L uciano Becchio firing the ball in
E ddie Lewis leaves to Derby
E veryone sad, 15 points away
D anger, Leeds are going up to the Championship
S uper Leeds rock the United Kingdom

U nited's Beckford is the hero
N o goals against them first seven games
I went to 24 out of 46 of them
T oo good for Southend and Port Vale
E ach player is so great
D oes it matter if Leeds don't go up? Yes it does!

George Cooper (8)
Menston Primary School, Menston

Dancing Stars

Have you ever seen stars dance?
I have: I once went up to space.
I saw some stars dancing, they were ace.

The stars dance gracefully,
They dance all night,
To the peaceful music, but not in sight.

The stars are so beautiful.
I hope one day you will be in my dreams,
Just to let you know the colour of the stars is cream.

Tarragon Huddleston (11)
Menston Primary School, Menston

Oh! Great Candy And Sweets

C aramel eggs with sprinkles.
A pple flavoured jelly lollies.
N ever eat fruit and veg, always eat candy.
D angerous, fizzy, gorgeous, delightful sweets.
Y ou could get hyper by eating candy.

S limy, stingy liquorice for the evening.
W icked sweets make you crazy.
E normous chocolate rabbits for Easter.
E xcellent Haribo for cinema.
T angy, toffee, tacky oranges.
S loppy, stretchy and dangly snakes.

William Hargreaves (8)
Menston Primary School, Menston

Winter

The ice, the ice
Slithery as a slimy slug
Look up, look down
Already shivering
Like mad

The icicles
Upside down
Like a mountain
Hanging and sparkling.

Ben Kirkham (8)
Menston Primary School, Menston

Let's Celebrate

It's that time of year,
When harvest is here.

Let's celebrate!

Crops growing fast,
With food to last.

Let's celebrate!

Storing the fare
For everyone to share.

Let's celebrate!

Emily Robson (9)
Menston Primary School, Menston

My Food For This Week

Monday I had spinach and leftover roast beef.
Tuesday I had chocolate and boiled red sweets.
Wednesday I had cheese on crackers but that I didn't like
so I snuck down stairs to get some cakes and biscuits.
Thursday I had spaghetti Bolognese but I pushed my
plate right away.
Friday I had bangers and mash but I put the mash in the trash.
Saturday it was meatballs. I was going to eat it but I had a big fall.
Sunday it was roast dinner that I find a delight but I threw a carrot
and started a fight.
But most of all out of every day I like my bedtime snack.

Kate Hargreaves (8)
Menston Primary School, Menston

The Storm

Dark clouds, swimming slowly across the grey sky
They bring hail, rain and destruction
Nothing can stop them.

Howling winds blow the trees, the people, and the Earth
Houses are blown away in the conquering gale
It's unstoppable.

The rain glistening in puddles on the ground,
It's just so shiny - like jewels falling from the sky
It soaks you to the skin - it just seems to go through everything
- the storm.

Gabriel O'Hooley (11)
Menston Primary School, Menston

Life At School

Life at school is really great,
But there's just one thing I hate,
It's not maths or literacy,
What it is is geography!
Life at school is really great
But geography's the thing I hate!

Josephine Gibbs (8)
Menston Primary School, Menston

School

S chool is fun
C lever it is
H elpful staff
O beying rules
O ver the top work
L oving school.

Daniel Aitken (7)
Menston Primary School, Menston

I Want To See Louise

I want to see Louise
Because all I ever see
Is muddy fields and trees
I hate peas but I love Louise
So please, please come Louise
Please come Louise please.

Rosie Brown (8)
Menston Primary School, Menston

Dragons

D ark as an evil wizard
R ed hot fire pouring from his mouth
A s big as a double decker bus
G reat, powerful and strong
O range like a setting sun
N oisy and roaring loudly.

Sam Gulley (9)
Menston Primary School, Menston

My Things

My lovely swimming pool is like a bright blue dream,
With a diving board in the Bahamas.

My gorgeous blue football boots are as brilliant as owning
The relaxing silky sea.

Jake Holberry (9)
Menston Primary School, Menston

Sports

Cricket and basketball
Or climbing the wall
Discus and football
And jumping in the Town Hall!

Rufus O'Hooley (8)
Menston Primary School, Menston

The Bet

He hits the ball in the net
The keeper could not save it
Fair and square he won the bet
At least he did his bit.

Daniel Ryan (10)
Menston Primary School, Menston

Hedgehog

My hedgehog is very pretty,
He always likes to play,
He rolls in a ball and gathers
Leaves along the way.

Molly Settle (8)
Menston Primary School, Menston

Snow

S now is good, snow is fun,
N ow you should start to run,
O n and on you should go,
W hite snow, watch it flow.

Fiona Moore (7)
Menston Primary School, Menston

Loving Someone

L ove is fantastic when you love someone
O ver the top when you love someone
V alentine's Day is great.
E xciting marriage.

Olivia Thomas (9)
Menston Primary School, Menston

The Underwater Adventure

Have you ever been under the sea?
Have you seen the same as me?
Well ...
Under the water and under the sea,
Lives a swiftly swimming seahorse.
With beautiful scales and a flowing tail
You can never be so happy to meet!

Have you ever been under the sea?
Have you see the same as me?
Well ...
Under the water and under the sea,
Lives a wonderful, whizzing whale.
With beady eyes and a swishing smile.
'Come swim along with me!'

Have you ever been under the sea?
Have you seen the same as me?
Well ...Under the water and under the sea,
Lives a fluttering, fancy flounder fish.
With its brilliant, brown body.
'Hey up mate? Come along?'

Have you ever been under the sea?
Have you seen the same as me?
Well ...
Under the water and under the sea
Lives a small, silky starfish.
With its tingling tentacles and slimy body.
'Come and sea bathe with me!'

Have you ever been under the sea?
Have you seen the same as me?
Well ...

Poetry Explorers – Yorkshire

Under the water and under the sea
Lives a frightening, ferocious shark.
With a crackling voice and a sweaty odour.
'Grrrr …You betta leave me alone!'

So you have seen what's under the sea?
But let's wait until next time …
Under the water and under the sea.

Amber Barratt (11)
Norton Community Primary School, Norton

Bad Dad

My dad was spinning and whirling,
Like a ballerina twirling,
It was all quite stunning,
As well as quite funny,
Then he went falling.

He got back up on his feet again,
And started dancing like a hen,
He was on one foot,
While chewing a nut,
Acting like drunk men.

After that he went to bed,
But when he went he bumped his head,
He found it quite fun,
'Till he was done,
Then he said
'Night-night.'

Anna Hubery (11)
Norton Community Primary School, Norton

Sharks Attacking

S wiftly swimming
H unting krill,
A ll are in fear,
R eefs are occupied,
K rill beware!
S tealthy sharks.

A mazingly attacking,
T errified triggerfish,
T remendous terror,
A ny area is unsafe,
C rabs crawling away,
K illing krill,
I mmense assault,
N othing to stop them!
G reat and mighty sharks.

Nathan Welham (10)
Norton Community Primary School, Norton

The Sun

I warm up the Earth.
I give out daylight.
The Earth turns away all sulky and miserable.
Then I am upset.
Twenty four hours later,
Earth comes back,
Then I am happy.

Harry Edwards (10)
Norton Community Primary School, Norton

Poetry Explorers – Yorkshire

The Monster!

Scary, large, green and tall,
You don't know what might happen
At Manor Hall!

Strange things occur at night,
It may jump out and give you a fright!

It's looking at you everywhere you go,
Look out kid you never know!

Walking above you walking behind you,
The noise it makes is high-pitch, 'Moo!'

Don't worry kid it's only a myth,
Even though it was quite realistic.

Adam Peel (10)
Norton Community Primary School, Norton

Man United

M en of wonder, walking to the theatre of dreams.
A bsolutely hammering every team that comes in their way.
N ani doing fantastic acrobatics.

U nited are we
N utty number seven goes to Heaven.
I mpeccable United scores another goal.
T evez tearing defenders apart.
E mbarrassing their opponents once again.
D iving opponents.

Marcus Brigham (11)
Norton Community Primary School, Norton

PS2 In Black

Play in the street,
Streets are black,
Two games in a ditch,
I look at them,
No it was the games of my dreams

Blind I went
Looks like a black oil spill
Simpson's book in a car
The car is red
It has large wheels
Red, red, everywhere I look
It's ... red!

Daniel Cockerill (11)
Norton Community Primary School, Norton

Yellow

I think of a summer's day, shining brightly.
A pool of happiness swirling around me.
Daffodils dancing dizzily in my dizzy dream.
Autumn leaves hanging from a lonely branch.
A buzzy bee flying around me.
Roses sat in a sunny window waiting to be spotted.
The planet of Saturn spinning in space.
The sun shining brightly on a summer's evening.

Grace Milner (10)
Norton Community Primary School, Norton

The Riddle

It's filled with life,
All tropical and wild,
The beauty of its amazing coloured coral.
With highly dangerous poison to kill,
Weird and wonderful things live here,
Many are helpful to others,
But the rest … I won't even say.

It's the star attraction of Australia,
So I'll say it now,
Do you know what I'm talking about?

A: The Great Barrier Reef.

Kieran Cook (10)
Norton Community Primary School, Norton

Red

A sign of love that lifts you up to a magical place,
Hatred looms lowly over your weary head,
The burning sun rolls around in the singing skies,
Embarrassment creeps up inside my body and reaches
                              my rosy cheeks,
A magical sign of romance with the indulging scent of roses
hovering carelessly like a bee,
A real ruby ring lays upon my wealthy finger.

Emma Piercy (10)
Norton Community Primary School, Norton

Purple

A fallen comrade on the golden sand,
The shouting and screaming in the back of your mind.

Tears falling down your face like a waterfall,
You carry on with the mental wounds in your head.

An oasis of freedom you desperately dream of,
The eerie spirit rises up the heavens of paradise.

The rushing adrenalin building up like a boat filling with deadly water,
That extra boost so you die a hero.

The pain as you fall to the silent sand,
Your chest is an ending pump.

Christopher Dean (10)
Norton Community Primary School, Norton

Pink

It is like a heart pouncing like a cheetah,
All the love is floating around in the air,
The roses are dancing as the wind sings his song,
As you sleep it brings happiness in your dreams,
The smooth songs playing in the distance,
All the diamonds glistening in the moonlight,
The love is spreading all around the world,
It will make all your dreams come true.

Jodie Hawes (11)
Norton Community Primary School, Norton

Wishes!

Looking into the distance, tears trickling down my rosy cheeks,
Swirling and dancing in my dreamy head,
Dreams crash to the floor like golden leaves falling off
                              a broken branch,
Excitement building up in my body,
Heart racing,
Smile forming,
Make-believe coming true.

Sophie Mort (10)
Norton Community Primary School, Norton

Happiness

It reminds me of a shining yellow sun, beating down in the
                              clear blue water.
A newborn baby seeing their first glimpse of their parents.
A rainbow's stripes lighting up the sky,
A freshly grown banana spreading its yellow glow,
A child's face after their first day at school,
This is what reminds me of happiness.

Charlotte Johnson (11)
Norton Community Primary School, Norton

Black

When you close your eyes the darkness takes over your body
Whilst walking through your dreams the dead of night closes in on you like a wave of darkness.
The midnight cat sits in the street with its glowing eyes as the moon shone down.
Loneliness is a cage trapping you inside forever from everyone in the world.

Lianna Hart (10)
Norton Community Primary School, Norton

My Rainbow

A burst of passion in the air above me.
A juicy orange waiting to be eaten in a fruit bowl.
A row of beautiful planted daffodils waiting to be picked.
Branches on a tree rustling in the night.
The sea at the seaside cold as can be.
A mum sitting in a fruit shop waiting to be seen.
Pink is the sign of love.

Lauren Clifford (10)
Norton Community Primary School, Norton

Poetry Explorers – Yorkshire

Gold

The sun beating down brightly on the autumn leaves.
Beautiful hair blowing carelessly in the breeze.
The tiny grains of sand in-between my ticklish toes.
A glint of hope shimmering in my eye.
Daffodils bobbing their heads on a summer's day.
A plane landing at a wondrous destination.
My head is filled with happy thoughts.

Rebekah Bell (11)
Norton Community Primary School, Norton

Yellow

A happy person on an enchanted walk to nowhere,
A rise of joy and gladness,
Bursts of light and excitement,
Warm and friendly heat,
Bright and loving daffodils swaying in the breeze,
Brilliant bright light from the stars above,
Happy shiny brightness in your eyes.

Imogen Barnes (10)
Norton Community Primary School, Norton

Black

It is like being all alone in an abandoned, dark room.
It is like killing one million innocent people.
It is like being chased by a pack of starving, wild dogs.
It is like getting in the middle of a guarded territory.
It is like entering a lair of mad most-wanted killers.
Hang-forth, for in the end I will die!

Caleb Barratt (11)
Norton Community Primary School, Norton

Night

Apprehensively, I trudge out into the deep, cold darkness.
Only a flickering light to guide me.
I feel headstrong, but the darkness grabs me like a soulless beast,
Not a glimpse of mercy in its eye.
Valiantly I carried on, and then a light shone from the distance.
I was free from my prison of darkness ...

Oscar Johnston (10)
Norton Community Primary School, Norton

Happy Horses

H appy horses grazing on the green, green grass.
O ver the field they prance and play.
R iding merrily round the countryside,
S un shining on their soft dappled coats.
E xercise is great fun, neighing all the way,
S ugar lumps to cheerfully munch on.

Kiera Colgan (11)
Norton Community Primary School, Norton

Poetry Explorers – Yorkshire

My Dog

My dog has an amazing smile,
Every day he chews on the ironing pile,
He has a white beard,
On it he has dog food smeared,
The only name for him is Harvey,
His favourite food is a carvery.

Nikita Daffern (11)
Norton Community Primary School, Norton

I'm King Of The City

Whenever people see me speeding past
They always shout, I wish I was that fast!
As I frantically pass every raggy old car in the city
I almost blow them away with my speed
That's why I'm king of the city.

Cameron Coulthard (10)
Norton Community Primary School, Norton

Moon

M oving around the Earth
O ver and over again
O rbiting the Earth every night
N ever ever stopping.

Stevie Hamilton (11)
Norton Community Primary School, Norton

Stars

S tars are like little lights in the sky
T winkling all night long
A nd on and on, shining so bright
R acing around like children
S taring down on the Earth.

Heather Robinson (10)
Norton Community Primary School, Norton

Silver

The shimmering sea, being shone on by the moon,
The soulless warrior fighting for his life,
The warrior's sword shining in the sun,
The miserable droplets of rain on the rough floor,
The light, lighting up the dark weary tunnel!

Rhys Douthwaite (11)
Norton Community Primary School, Norton

Red

It reminds me of love.
It's danger warning me.
Anger is a large bowl of blood.
It's a heart beating mad in me.
It's victory from a battlefield at the end of the war.

Joshua Downing (10)
Norton Community Primary School, Norton

Magical, Wonderful Earwax

Earwax isn't bad -
However you may please
Even if it looks like melted Cheddar cheese!

It comes in metric tonnes
It lives inside your ear.
If we didn't have wax
Then we wouldn't be here!

The thicker sticky wax
Are back-up reinforcements.
If intruders get inside
Your head - now that's importance!

The wax does have clothes -
Yellow, orange, green.
If you have long hair,
Then it renders unseen!

But when the ear's washed
The wax droops like a flower
It's losing all its stamina
It's losing all its power.

The wax seems very lonely;
Will you give him a friend?
Now listen very closely -
The story's coming to an end.

The wax wants to be happy
Like everyone in the world
And like everyone else
Doesn't want to be treated like mould.

Joseph Wing (11)
St Mary's RC Primary School, Malton

The Day And Night

In the morning at the dawn of day,
Why do all the birds fly away?
In the mist all blue and grey,
The wild tiger looks for prey.

At midday all the colours are bright,
And the squirrels and the rabbits come into sight,
All the sun shines and everything is light,
And the birds fly around like a soaring kite.

At midnight when the moon shines,
And the crickets do their whine,
The horizon has its perfect line,
And the clock strikes 12 and starts to chime.

Ellen Longworth (10)
St Mary's RC Primary School, Malton

Snow

Snow falls down,
Upon the town.
It's white and gentle,
When a strong wind blows it's mental.

Floating down in a big white gown,
Some people smile, some people frown.
But when the sun comes out,
Without a doubt, it melts!

Mary Rice (10)
St Mary's RC Primary School, Malton

The Eye Of London

The all-seeing eye of London
Stands, guarding the River Thames
Doing endless cartwheels for the public's own amusement
Its arms protecting people from the outside world
Slow as a tortoise, the magnificent wheel slowly revolves
The Tower Bridge overseeing the task
It works busily, all day, and at night, it whispers the same word
Over and over again:
'Slave, slave, slave …'

Thomas Wing (11)
St Mary's RC Primary School, Malton

Snow

Falling from the sky like tiny wedding veils,
Thinking it's the end for them
Only to land on soft tickly grass.
But they don't stay the same, oh no
They fly around in groups and crash into children
But when the sun comes out, it's time for the snow to go
Until the winter comes again.

Callum Young (11)
St Mary's RC Primary School, Malton

Haiku

A haiku is strange
Five syllables then seven
Then it's five, how strange.

Daniela Horne (11)
St Mary's RC Primary School, Malton

Football Rap

This is the box,
And we are the knocks,
So here comes the football,
And this is your shot.

Here comes the football,
Zooming up the field,
Better kick it up,
Or you're gonna squeal.

Squeal if you like,
This is not a fight,
So pick up your gloves,
That is what we like.

Liking is good,
Good is what we like,
Kick it in the net,
Then jump with delight.

Joe Harrison (10)
St Peter's RC Primary School, Scarborough

Poetry Explorers – Yorkshire

The Big Book Of Bees

A small little boy
He saw a big book
And said to his sister
Come and take a look!

So they looked in the book
With a girl called Ruth Cook
And they sat on a chair
In the shape of a pear.

And what did they see?
A ginormous big bee!
It flew round and round
But it fell on the ground.

Another man came
And saw the bee sight
Got a hole in his belly
Ooh what a fright!

Rebecca Guy came
And Jenny Scott too
They laughed and laughed
So much that they needed the loo!

Oops, whoops!
Oh now what's happened?
Nobody's there
They will have left in a wagon!

So he got on his bike
And chased after them
And as he passed by
He saw a big hen!

Oh where have you been?
We've been in a cave!
So that's where you've been
You've got to behave!
Bee happy!

Georgia Ward (9)
St Peter's RC Primary School, Scarborough

School Is Boring

School is boring,
School is boring,
You never get to draw,
A fun old drawing.

At break,
At break,
If you're asleep,
You have to wake.

The toast,
The toast,
It's always wiped,
On a dirty post.

On the table there are bogies,
On the table there are bogies,
All from the school
St Ogies.

The dinners are slop,
The dinners are slop,
I think after this,
I'll need a plop.

The teachers are dumb,
The teachers are dumb,
They always point with,
Their thumb.

There are frogs,
There are frogs,
Every day they make,
Their own bog.

The head teacher,
The head teacher,
Does not know
What is a feature.

Poetry Explorers – Yorkshire

St Peter's is great,
St Peter's is great,
They've never had a child,
Ever faint.

So don't go to school,
Apart from St Peter's,
Because if you go to any other,
You will be a fool!

Alex Duncan (10)
St Peter's RC Primary School, Scarborough

The Ghost

Little Mary of nine.
Was feeling fine
Until she saw a ghost
That scared her the most.

Oh that terrible ghost,
Oh that terrible ghost,
It scared her the most,
But it wasn't that scary …

It made her wonder what it could be
What could it be?
What could it be?

A week later it came again,
Under the mat it sat
Mary lifted the mat
To find it was Molly her cat!

Abigail Kimmitt (9)
St Peter's RC Primary School, Scarborough

Good And Bad, Right And Wrong!

Good and bad,
Right and wrong,
If you want to stay safe,
Listen to our song!

If you're hit by a car,
You'll fly so far,
So look left and right,
And you won't have a fright!

Good and bad,
Right and wrong,
If you want to stay safe,
Listen to our song!

If it's not bright,
Wear something light,
So be safe and be seen,
And the drivers won't be mean!

Good and bad,
Right and wrong,
If you want to stay safe,
Listen to our song!

Don't drink and drive,
We want to stay alive,
So stop and think,
You could go before you think.

James Brown (10)
St Peter's RC Primary School, Scarborough

Year 5 Rules

Year 5 rules
Year 5 is the best
The best in the school,
Don't think about the rest.

Everyone has a friend,
A friend is good,
My friend Joe,
He is the best and he rules.

Ebin just left us,
He really rocked.
We made a card for him,
He loved it so much,
He took it home with him,
And he always remembered us.

His-toric, His-toric,
His-torical day,
That's what we had on Friday.
Fri-Fris name is Ryan
Friday he hates,
Because he gets fried.

James Pilmer (10)
St Peter's RC Primary School, Scarborough

My Friends

My friends are great
One makes a debate
My friends are cool
One has a pool
My friends are brill
One gives me the chill
My friends are ace
One player's the base
My friends are happy
One wears a nappy
My friends are nice
One loves rice
My friends are funny
One hops like a bunny
My friends are kind
One is blind
My friends are weird
One grows a beard
My friends are brave
One wears aftershave.

Matthew Cottle (10)
St Peter's RC Primary School, Scarborough

When I Looked Over The Hedge

When I looked over the hedge,
I saw a unicorn!
I looked to see if there was anything else
But then I spotted a little fawn.

When I looked over the hedge,
I saw a lady knitting,
What she was knitting it looked very nice
Then I realised it was a mitten.

When I looked over the hedge,
I saw a fish swimming in a bowl
I looked away then I looked back
And the fish had gone down a hole!

When I looked over the hedge
I felt the sun shining on my face
I looked at the pond
And I saw the swans swimming with grace.

Ella Gridley (10)
St Peter's RC Primary School, Scarborough

About Matthew

My friend's Matthew
He's football crazy
He's better than the rest
And never lazy.

He's got a friend
She's Chloe Moran
She is lovely
And has a tan.

He loves Liverpool
And computer games too
He has a Game Boy
And a PlayStation 2

He's got another friend
His name is Liam
He has an Xbox
And comes round to see him.

Jacob Ratcliffe (9)
St Peter's RC Primary School, Scarborough

My Class

My class are caring,
They are always sharing,
My class are fab,
But some of them are mad!

My class are loving,
They are never shoving,
My class are great,
But they can be really late.

Becky is really funny
And she really likes honey
Becky is really kind
I would never leave her behind.

Georgia's nickname is Chowder,
I don't think anyone could be louder,
Georgia's really funny,
She wants to be a bunny!

Jenny Scott (9)
St Peter's RC Primary School, Scarborough

My Garden

In my garden there is,
Butterflies, bees and even fish!
And when I go out to play,
I have fun and stay out all day!

In my garden I play lots of games,
So I threw a ball, but it hit the windowpanes!
My mum never knew,
Which I'm glad of too!

I play a game called hopscotch,
I thought it was getting late, so I looked at my watch!
Luckily it wasn't, so I went in the shed,
But then I tripped over and bumped my head!

In the garden, my mum came running out,
'Are you OK, are you OK?' she began to shout!
We rushed to hospital, my mum and me,
I think she took it too seriously!

Rebecca Guy (10)
St Peter's RC Primary School, Scarborough

Poetry Explorers – Yorkshire

My Raindrop

My dog is like a raindrop
Sitting by the door
Everybody loves him
I couldn't love him more.

I take him for a walk every single day
We go to the park for a little play
He really loves the hay
He also loves to lay.

I love him with my heart
I can't stand it when we're apart
He's barking mad even
When he's sad.

Scott Brierley (10)
St Peter's RC Primary School, Scarborough

One Cold Night

One cold night I saw a shadow in front of me
What on Earth could it be?
It made me scared it made me wonder
Then it started to thunder
One cold night I saw a shape in front of me
What on Earth could it be?
It made me worried, it gave me a pain then it started to rain
One cold night I saw a figure
Then I realised I was looking in the mirror.

Tiffany Harrison (10)
St Peter's RC Primary School, Scarborough

A Dog Like No Other

(Inspired by 'I Stood By Your Bed Last Night' by Anon)

Winner

I sat by your bed last night, you found it hard to sleep,
I laid my paws on your bed, just to have a peep,
I really wanted to comfort you, as you wiped away a tear,
'I'm not gone, don't be sad, I am here.'

We went for a wander by the park, my favourite place to be,
We went for a stroll by the ducks, I always loved to see,
But when we went to my grave, a tear trickled down your cheek,
I felt so sad and guilty, my own eyes started to weep.

I really wanted to stay with you, but I knew you couldn't see me,
I will always be by your side, yes I will always be,
And the other night just us two, I heard you quietly mutter,
'He really truly was a dog like no other.'

Chloé Moran (10)
St Peter's RC Primary School, Scarborough

The Naughty Boy

There once was a naughty boy, sitting on a chair.
He had a lunch but he didn't want to share.
He saw a tunnel and he looked at the bat.
When he saw the big rock, he sat.
The next day, there was a new kid at school,
So he bullied him because he was cool.

Michelle Sunico (10)
St Peter's RC Primary School, Scarborough

Football Mad

Fred was football mad,
He also had a crazy dad,
He always wore his Chelsea shirt,
And he always got covered in dirt.
One day his dad took him to a game,
Fred's favourite player was Frank Lampard that was his name

Chelsea were playing Man U, any way they suck,
They always play like a duck!
Lampard was going up the field, Man U were playing like a mole!
Lampard shot and he scored a goal!
Chelsea were playing Man U, anyway, they suck,
They always play like a duck!

Angus Polkey (10)
St Peter's RC Primary School, Scarborough

The Footie Friend

I have this new friend.
He says we'll be mates till the end,
But when I give him a call,
All he talks about is football!

Who won on Saturday?
How did they play?
Did Gerrard score?
What a win eh!

That's all he sings,
'You'll Never Walk Alone,' It gives me nightmares.
Like kissing Kylie Minogue!

Eleanor Regan (10)
St Peter's RC Primary School, Scarborough

Bumblebee

B umblebees are yellow and black.
U nkind creatures.
M y mum screams when she sees a bee.
B ad bees, if you break their house they go mad.
L ovely and bright.
E very summer they come out.
B ees suck the honey out of flowers.
E yes are black.
E at nectar.

Sophie Walker (9)
Southcoates Primary School, Hull

Bumblebee

B ig and buzzy.
U nhappy every time.
M umbling all the time.
B lack and yellow.
L ovely and yellowy bright.
E very time they are buzzing.
B eautiful in every way.
E very day they come out in summer.
E very day they collect honey.

Hannah Townend (7)
Southcoates Primary School, Hull

Ladybird

L ittle legs crawling across the floor.
A cross the garden into its den.
D ay after day, munching and crunching.
Y ears go by, ladybirds die.
B aby ladybirds learn new things.
I love ladybirds.
R ed body shines bright.
D ots all over their bodies.

Amy Watkin (9)
Southcoates Primary School, Hull

Football – Haikus

Football is great fun.
I love football it is great.
Because it is fun.

I support team Hull.
I play for a football team.
Football is the best.

Shanice Bell (8)
Southcoates Primary School, Hull

Butterfly Kennings

Garden flyer
Six legs
Nectar eater
Many eyes
Garden liker
Fast flyer.

Connor Thompson (8)
Southcoates Primary School, Hull

Ladybird – Haiku

Spotted ladybird
Quickly flying round the sky
Fly high in the sky.

Ellie Danville (8)
Southcoates Primary School, Hull

The Sun – Haiku

The sun shines on me
The sun is full of goodness
The sun gives us light.

Jessica Wilkinson (9)
Southcoates Primary School, Hull

Parents

Parents make me rather sad
Sometimes they make me mad,
At school they embarrass me
Come to the gate and you will see,
At night they say goodnight and I snuggle down and can't
                                                                               get to sleep
Last night I didn't sleep a peep,
In the morning I get dressed
But I want to have a rest.

When my friends come to play
We have some fun anyway,
But when they're gone it's time to say
You embarrassed me all day,
This is the end of today,
I'll read it again another day.

Megan Idle
Stakesby Primary School, Whitby

Monkeys

M onkeys are stupid all the time.
O ne morning bananas grew off a vine.
N ow it is summer they like to hide.
K icking each other two by two.
E very day babies come through.
Y esterday one just died.
S o little babies please go and hide.

Alfie Swales
Stakesby Primary School, Whitby

The Monster

I saw it in the night,
It was a monster,
I swear,
It ran from side to side,
And it looked like a bear.

It was hairy and big,
And it had a great nose,
Then it started to dig,
And spray water out the hose.

Calm down dear,
It was only your dad,
But I tell you it was big and bad.

Yasmin Dimbleby (8)
Stakesby Primary School, Whitby

The Mischievous Monkey

Monkeys are annoying,
But not as annoying as the mischievous monkey,
He jumps on your head and skydives off,
He bites your nose,
And worst of all, he throws banana skins at you,
So watch out for that mischievous monkey
He might be hanging around your house one day.

Tilly Swales (9)
Stakesby Primary School, Whitby

Flower

Growing and growing in the garden,
Smell the lovely, lovely smell.
Watch the flower grow,
Growing and growing so it is very tall,
It's the tallest you have ever seen before,
It's taller than you; it's taller than you
But it is not taller than me!

Charlotte Wharrick (9)
Stakesby Primary School, Whitby

My Dog Is . . .

My dog is mad,
My dog is funny,
My dog is black and as sweet as honey,
My dog is as soft as a bunny and knows that we love her,
My dog is mad,
My dog is funny,
And she knows that she is as sweet as honey!

Helena Graham (9)
Stakesby Primary School, Whitby

My Dad's Shoe

My dad's shoe, it stinks so bad,
It smells like a horse's hoof
When it's stepped in a cowpat.
One time I sniffed it,
I don't know why
And now I have to wear a gas mask
All the time!

Henry Atkinson (9)
Stakesby Primary School, Whitby

Kittens

K ittens are very, very cute and cuddly.
I n the night they might miaow gently.
T hey love being tickled under the chin.
T hey like to run round their muddy garden.
E at up, eat up, eat your meaty food.
N o! Don't scratch the wallpaper.
S nuggle up you little rascal.

Amy Porteus (9)
Stakesby Primary School, Whitby

Family

F unny people.
A ll my family is nice.
M y family loves me.
I love my family.
L oving is in my family.
Y ou love your family.

Joe Beeforth (9)
Stakesby Primary School, Whitby

Happy

H appy people are all around the world,
A ngry people are still happy,
P eople are always happy,
P eople are sometimes happy and sometimes angry.
Y ou need to be happy all the time!

Fleur Waring (8)
Stakesby Primary School, Whitby

Happy

H appy people all around.
A ngry people make lots of sounds.
P eople are having lots of fun.
P eople like having sleepovers all around the world.
Y ou need to feel happy all the time.

Kaitlin Swales
Stakesby Primary School, Whitby

From A Railway Carriage

From a railway carriage I can see
An amazing icy loch with an island
With a gigantic castle in the middle.

From my railway carriage I can see
A meadow with the most beautiful daisies, cattle too.

From my railway carriage I can see
An amazing view from up in the mountains,
Over the hills, meadows, rivers and ditches.

From my railway carriage I can see
A lake which I would call Swan Lake,
With beautiful amazing swans on top.

From my railway carriage I can see
A beautiful old tree as big as a skyscraper.

From my railway carriage I can see
A wonderful river running through the forest.

From my railway carriage I can see
A small brown duckling glimmering in the sun.

From my railway carriage I can see
A horse race and I hope the red one wins.

From my railway carriage I can see
A lovely lagoon shining in the sun.

Jake Brown (8)
Swainby & Potto CE Primary School, Swainby

Explore!

I step onto the sand and start to explore,
In a new place and country that I have never been to before.

I lay down in the sun and put on my lotion,
Take off my flip-flops and go jump in the ocean.

The ocean greets me with a calming, soothing, breeze,
The water is now up to my head not my knees.

As I take to the plunge into the sea,
Bright tropical fish swim by and welcome me.

I swim to a cave that's all glossy inside,
I hear the gurgle of fish and the swoosh of the tide.

I lay down to relax outside the cave in the sun,
I start to think about everything, and all I have done.

I sit up to check the atmosphere around,
The water, the fish and silence surrounds.

I decide to swim back for I have to go on a plane,
A new place and new country to do everything again.

Bethany Morgan (11)
Swainby & Potto CE Primary School, Swainby

Eagle – Haiku

Soaring in the air
Flying for his meaty prey
Then stabbing like knives.

Ryan Beadle (10)
Swainby & Potto CE Primary School, Swainby

From My Railway Carriage

From my railway carriage I can see
A frozen, shiny, magnificent lake
With swans skidding across.

From a railway carriage I can see
Massive green moor-tops stretching for miles
And plants rustling in the wind.

From a railway carriage I can see
A bright red tractor passing by
With a haystack on the back.

From a railway carriage I can see
Bright yellow meadows that look like a golden carpet.

From a railway carriage I can see
Huge glistening mansions that look like sparkling diamonds.

From a railway carriage I can see
Cute fluffy sheep looking at me,
Chomping on a bit of grass.

Jona Turner (9) & William Howes (11)
Swainby & Potto CE Primary School, Swainby

From A Railway Carriage

From my railway carriage I can see
Huge flats and nice houses.
From my railway carriage I can see
Cool motorbikes, black and red cars and bikes
With drink holders.
From my railway carriage I can see
Lots of hotels and tall hills which were really high.
From my railway carriage I can see
A stinky zoo with stinky animals in the rivers and cages.
From my railway carriage I can see
A great field with tractors and diggers.
From my railway carriage I can see
A large school with little and big children playing.
From my railway carriage I can see
A frozen pond with jumping frogs and ice.
From my railway carriage I can see
A city road with a noisy traffic jam.

Thomas Stevens (9)
Swainby & Potto CE Primary School, Swainby

From A Railway Carriage

From a railway carriage I can see
A glittering lake,
A beautiful snowy mountain.
From a railway carriage I can see
Some gleaming red apples
From a railway carriage I can see
Cows chomping away on razor green grass
Jockeys riding their horses to the stable
From a railway carriage I can see
A passing train
'Oh look there's someone waving to me,'
From a railway carriage I can see
An old crooked tramp eating a cheese and onion pasty
From a railway carriage I can see
Two cute baby Labradors lost and cold
Bushes and hedges with prickly leaves on them.

Joe McKenna (7)
Swainby & Potto CE Primary School, Swainby

Poetry Explorers — Yorkshire

From My Railway Carriage . . .

From my railway carriage I can see,
Some red, juicy apples on a tall apple tree
And a rabbit hopping round its burrow,
Like someone who's lost their key,
From my railway carriage I can see,
A tall smooth hill, like where I once went skiing and
Someone's at the top now - dancing with glee.
From my railway carriage I can see,
Another train passing by, hey! Someone's waving at me!
And there's my friend's mum, sipping tea.
There's so many things for you to see,
Just hop on a train, honestly,
It's really worth your tiny fee!

Kate Stevens (11)
Swainby & Potto CE Primary School, Swainby

From My Railway Carriage

From my railway carriage I can see
A rippling river, horrible litter and strong
Safe fences looking after the animals.
From my railway carriage I can see
Woolly, thick, white sheep munching on juicy grass,
Muddy slimy pigs rolling in the wet mud
And cute little puppies with their mums on a tiring walk.
From my railway carriage I can see
A beautiful sunset going down behind the hills.
From my railway carriage I can see
A twiggy bird's nest with feathery birds sat in the nest.
From my railway carriage I can see
Other speedy trains passing by extremely fast.

Elle Harrison (8)
Swainby & Potto CE Primary School, Swainby

From A Railway Carriage

From my railway carriage I can see
Giant trees with yellow crinkly leaves
Bristly bushes when the whistling wind blows
And wooden cottages blowing in the wind.

From my railway carriage I can see
A deep frosty lake with ice and slush on
An old man with a pet rabbit in a cage
A big deer in the woods and a baby deer with her mother.

From my railway carriage I can see
A horse chomping on the yellow hay
Some cows crunching the green, green grass
A farmer in a farm milking a black and white cow.

Jade Keetley (8)
Swainby & Potto CE Primary School, Swainby

Poetry Explorers – Yorkshire

From My Railway Carriage

From my railway carriage I can see
Some glittering shiny water
As I eat my chocolate it gets shorter and shorter.
From my railway carriage I can see
Some animals hopping all around the fields.
In the river there are some big eels.
From my railway carriage I can see
Some woolly, fluffy sheep in the meadow
And some beautiful cities and some lovely houses.
From my railway carriage I can see
Some little scratching running mice.

Zoe Ralston (10)
Swainby & Potto CE Primary School, Swainby

Volcano

Lava spitting out
The volcano is erupting
It is dark and misty
The floor is shaking
Volcano, volcano don't erupt
I don't know what to do
Lava flows from house to house
Run, run don't look back
My house is ruined, I feel so sad
We thought it was dormant
But it erupted instead.

Kyra Pymer (10)
Thorpepark Primary School, Hull

Volcano

A volcano banging
People running
Everyone going
The lava's coming.

The volcano is bubbling
It is as hot as the sun
It sounds as if it's drumming
Watch out everyone the lava is about to come!

The lava is as fast as a cheetah
It's a huge destroyer
You better watch out before it gets you
It's an enormous rock thrower.

Danielle Johnson (10)
Thorpepark Primary School, Hull

Volcanoes Erupt

V olcanoes erupt
O ut from the sky is lava
L ava is hot
C rater is lava flowing
A sh clouds fill the air
N othing comes out, then it is dormant
O ut only on top of the volcano
E ruption clouds
S moke fills the air.

Luke Hall (10)
Thorpepark Primary School, Hull

A Fearful Destroyer!

Town-disturber
Lava-spewer
Smoke-puffer
Rock-thrower
Human-killer
Land-maker
Powerful-erupter
Deadly-exploder
Active-spitter
Magma-shooter
Life-taker
A fearful destroyer.

Dana Lowther (10)
Thorpepark Primary School, Hull

A Volcano

Ash-thrower
Lava-spitter
Smoke-spinner
House-destroyer
Rock-firer
Lava-shooter
Human-murderer
Crime-creator
Crater-cracker
Crop-grower.

Scott Morfitt (10)
Thorpepark Primary School, Hull

Volcano

Volcanoes are tall
The lava shoots out
If it erupted I would shout.

Some volcanoes are small
The rocks rumble
Mainly them all
And they tumble.

The people are scared
The children play with their toys
Because they heard
A rumbling noise.

Shannon Heath (10)
Thorpepark Primary School, Hull

Volcano

Hot-lava
Big-chamber
Ash-maker
Loud-sound
Smoky-vents
Rocky-hill
Boiling-crater
Dormant-volcano
Streaming-lava
It's a bad day!

Macauley Watts (9)
Thorpepark Primary School, Hull

Poetry Explorers – Yorkshire

Volcano

Lava-squirter
Rock-thrower
Ash-hurdler
Smoke-spreader
Landscape-burner
People-killer
Loud-rumbler
Magma-shooter
Land-former
A volcano.

Cameron Waters (10)
Thorpepark Primary School, Hull

Volcano

Hot lava
Black cloud
Yellow sparks
Red lava
Bubbling magma
Pumice maker
Lava flow
Smoky air
Boiling ash
Death causer.

Adam Rumkee (11)
Thorpepark Primary School, Hull

Volcanoes

Hot lava
Bubbling magma
Ash pouring
Eroding away
Active Versuvius
Smoky air
Rocky mountain
Black clouds
Enormous bang
Crater edge.

Nathan Lawler (10)
Thorpepark Primary School, Hull

Volcano

Hot, lava
Smoky, vent
Pumice, rocky
Bubbly, magma
Volcanologist, work,
Crater, enormous
Massive, chamber
Dormant, volcano
Ash, pumice
It is erupting!

Jade Jackson (11)
Thorpepark Primary School, Hull

Poetry Explorers — Yorkshire

Volcano

Vicious-thrower
Volcano-erupter
Lava-glower
Town-beater
People-hater
Lava-flower
Mountain-blower
Crater-exploding
A murderous thing.

Matthew Richards (10)
Thorpepark Primary School, Hull

Mount St Helens

Mount St Helens is very deadly,
It's going to erupt soon,
Oh no! Someone shouted
Then it went *kaboom!*

It was erupting even more,
They all had to go,
Ash is scattered everywhere,
Then they saw the lava flow.

Ellie Humphrey (10)
Thorpepark Primary School, Hull

An Unfriendly Volcano

Vicious
Lava flowing,
Red hot magma
Blowing off its top.
Rocks making a cracking sound,
It's erupting with a deafening bang!
Lava killing everyone who's in its way.

Joanne Charlton (11)
Thorpepark Primary School, Hull

Volcano

V olcano erupting
O verflow
L ava pouring
C louds of smoke
A cross mountain
N asty volcano
O ngoing eruption.

Jordan Hall (10)
Thorpepark Primary School, Hull

Our Senses

Out at the end of town
Where you can hear the leaves rattle

In the wind at night
When the moon starts to rise

You can see the snow falling
On the frozen path

When you are sitting on your couch
Looking out of the window

While you are eating a bar of chocolate
And drinking some coffee

In the morning when the sun
Is shining bright

When you are laid on the beach
You can hear the waves smashing together

In the winter when you walk in the street
And hear the crunchy noises you make

When you get snuggled into bed
And feel warm at night

When you touch snow
It feels like your hand freezes like ice

You have five different senses
And you use them in your own way.

Georgie Taylor & Kara Calvert (10)
Tilbury Primary School, Hull

Smoke Alarms Save Lives

S moke alarms save lives.
M atches set things on fire.
O ver 360 people get killed by rubbish fires.
K ill! Kill! That's what the fire does.
E ngines come as quick as they can.

A lert! Alert! The fire is coming
L ights flashing like mad in the middle of the night
A larms going off to save our lives.
R escue! Rescue! The firefighters go in,
M e and my family in a safe home.

Bethany Harper & Hollie Toft (10)
Tilbury Primary School, Hull

Living Hell

Living Hell
Hell is fiery like chilli
And hot like boiling water
Hell is evil
And like death
Hell is the opposite of nice
Satan is cruel like a stubborn dragon
I wish I'd been good on Earth.

Oliver Bradley (9), Owen Fullard & Matthew Burgess (10)
Tilbury Primary School, Hull

My Friendship Token Poem

Friendship means a lot to me!
My friends and I sit on the sofa and have a cup of tea.
So come and stay with me.

Elisha-Mae Jones (9)
Tilbury Primary School, Hull

Young Writers Information

We hope you have enjoyed reading this book - and that you will continue to enjoy it in the coming years.

If you like reading and writing poetry drop us a line, or give us a call, and we'll send you a free information pack.

Alternatively if you would like to order further copies of this book or any of our other titles, then please give us a call or log onto our website at www.youngwriters.co.uk

Young Writers Information
Remus House
Coltsfoot Drive
Peterborough
PE2 9JX
(01733) 890066